TOWARD LIQUOR CONTROL

TOWARD LIQUOR CONTROL

By
Raymond B. Fosdick
and
Albert L. Scott

With a Foreword by
John D. Rockefeller, Jr.

Introduction By
Jim Petro
Brannon P. Denning
Jim Hall
Patrick Lynch
Jerry Oliver
Board of Advisors, Center for Alcohol Policy

TOWARD LIQUOR CONTROL

About The Center for Alcohol Policy

The mission of the Center is to educate policy makers, regulators
and the public about alcohol, its uniqueness and its regulation. By
conducting sound research and implementing initiatives that maintain
appropriate state-based regulation of alcohol, the Center promotes
safe and responsible consumption of alcohol, fights underage drinking
and drunk driving and informs the key entities and the public
about the effects of alcohol consumption.
Visit www.centerforalcoholpolicy.org to learn more.

1101 King Street
Suite 600 A
Alexandria, VA 22314
www.centerforalcoholpolicy.org

Cover Photographs Courtesy of Library of Congress Public Collection

978-0-9833007-0-0

CONTENTS

INTRODUCTION

FOSDICK AND SCOTT'S *TOWARD LIQUOR CONTROL* HAS DONE MORE TO SHAPE modern American alcohol policy than any other book except the Bible.

Attempting to describe what *Toward Liquor Control* teaches reminds us of a 1980's television commercial for Prego spaghetti sauce with its tagline "It's in there." What about meat? It's in there. What about spices? It's in there. And so on.

For anyone who has ever wondered how America's alcohol regulatory systems were created, how they have worked, and why they have stood the test of time, "It's in there" best summarizes *Toward Liquor Control*. Ask a series of questions about important historical and recurring alcohol policies and the answer is the same: "It's in there."

Does *Toward Liquor Control* explain why Prohibition failed? It's in there. What are the dangers of bootleggers and lack of respect for the law? In there. Does it explain why alcohol manufacturers should not own retailers? Does it discuss alcohol taxation? State run liquor stores? Why lower alcohol products like beer and wine should be regulated differently than hard liquor? Political activities by the alcohol industry? The need for strong and independent state alcohol regulators? Tied house laws? Alcohol advertising? The problems of drunk driving and growing use of specialty mechanical operations? The need for, but limits of, education relating to alcohol and its use? It's all in there. Items that this book addresses are still relevant to modern policy debates.

And even items that are not specifically mentioned in *Toward Li-*

quor Control are "in there." For example, this book serves as a road map for many modern issues facing policy makers even beyond alcohol. Whether it is regulation of newer types of alcohol products, marijuana legalization, or the limits of education campaigns, *Toward Liquor Control* serves as a fountain of knowledge and direction for all who drink from its pages.

Because of its historical importance and its timeless relevance, this book is a must read for anyone interested in today's alcohol regulatory system. It was commissioned by John D. Rockefeller, Jr., who admitted that Prohibition, his preferred policy, embodied in the 18th Amendment, was a failure; but rather than throwing up his hands, he rolled up his sleeves and funded this seminal work to serve as a blueprint for what would happen when alcohol was again legal.

As Rockefeller notes in his foreword, "Except to ask Mr. Fosdick and Mr. Scott to make the investigation, I have taken no part in the matter." And he made great selections with Raymond B. Fosdick, a practicing attorney who was already an expert on police and international matters and Albert L. Scott, an engineer, who was active in social and religious movements including Alcoholics Anonymous.

Fosdick and Scott published *Toward Liquor Control* in 1933, just as the 21st Amendment was being ratified. Their comprehensive study arrived just in time to bridge the divide between "wets" and "drys" as they created a new alcohol policy. It helped create a permanent peace between these groups whose members had battled for decades in local municipal elections all the way to presidential platform committees. Alcohol was the defining political issue for countless elections and many parts of the country had swung between dry and wet like a piano metronome with the loser stewing and plotting their next attempt to swing the debate their way. *Toward Liquor Control* broke this metronomic cycle by creating a new template to shape future political, legislative and economic debates about alcohol and its role in society. Stability was a new concept to be tested.

Toward Liquor Control's four main themes remain relevant today:

- It expresses strong support for the state serving as the seller of alcohol over the license system. The book asserts that a state run system would prevent the gradual erosion of alcohol controls by those with economic interests in the alcohol business.
- It strongly pushes for trade practice regulations and the prevention of vertical integration in the alcohol market. Alcohol regulation should also ensure the continued absence of the saloon from American social life.
- It notes that states must use their control systems to steer society to lower alcohol form of products. Liquor is to be tightly restricted; lower forms of alcohol such as lower alcohol beer and wines are to have less restrictive regulations. It notes that the return of beer early in 1933 did not create problems and should serve as a model for lower alcohol products; and
- It notes the limits of theoretical and utopian ideals as a way to regulate society. There must be political support the authors concluded:

Forty eight states are attempting to set up a new method of control. In the last analysis, there is but one fundamental rule to be followed-and all other rules are corollaries: If the new system is not rooted in what the people of each state sincerely desire at this moment, it makes no difference how logical and complete it may appear as a statute – it cannot succeed.

There are many other important points relating to the proper level of taxation, both of the product and the industry, education, the best type of license systems, political influence by the alcohol industry, and education programs by government entities. Many of these points remain relevant and timely discussion items to this date.

However, it must also be noted what is <u>not</u> in *Toward Liquor Control*. Many important regulatory functions were developed after this book as state governments put the theories of *Toward Liquor*

Control into practice by standing up strong working alcohol regulatory systems. The state governments later created systems and eventually the use of words such as "three tier" and "wholesaler" grew out of these next steps. Obviously this 1933 book could not predict specific modern alcohol debates about the internet, new alcoholic products, ignition interlock devices or other policy debates that have commanded attention recently. However, its general guides do offer assistance even in today's debates.

Toward Liquor Control makes the case for the system that has become today's successful, state-based regulatory system. This book takes the important perspective that regardless of the authors' personal opinions, alcohol will now be legal—so how does society make sure this historically problematic and controversial issue is regulated? How does a society regulate an industry that has a proven track record of being irresponsible? How do you regulate a product that in moderation produces social ease and possibly even some medical benefits, while in excess causes serious societal and physiological harm? How do you apply laws of economics to a product, unlike other consumer goods, whose ubiquity and low price are causes for concern? Fosdick and Scott anticipated these recurring problems and provided a road map to provide guidance to policymakers, regulators, control advocates, industry stakeholders and the public.

The book asks and answers a number of important questions that were important in 1933 and remain important today. The Center for Alcohol Policy believes that this book has been out of modern policy discussions far too long. The Center seeks to get this important work into the hands of academics, policy makers, regulators, and anyone else interested in debates about alcohol. The same issues identified by Fosdick and Scott in the 1930's are still being discussed today. The Center for Alcohol Policy is pleased make this book widely available. We hope it contributes to both a better understanding of existing state alcohol policies as well as informing the ongoing debate over the future of those policies.

We strongly believe that you should read *Toward Liquor Con-*

trol, draw your own conclusions and marvel at its relevance today. We believe that no matter what your perspective or policy interest, when searching for answers you will agree, "It's in there."

> *Sincerely,*
> Jim Petro, *Former Attorney General of Ohio*
>
> Brannon P. Denning, *Professor of Law, Cumberland School of Law, Samford University*
>
> Jim Hall, *Former Chairman, National Transportation Safety Board*
>
> Patrick Lynch, *Former Attorney General of Rhode Island*
>
> Jerry Oliver, *Former Chief of Police and Former Director Arizona Liquor License and Control*

FOREWORD
By
John D. Rockefeller, Jr.

I was born a teetotaler and I have been a teetotaler on principle all my life. Neither my father nor his father ever tasted a drop of intoxicating liquor. I could hope that the same might be true of my children and their children. It is my earnest conviction that total abstinence is the wisest, best, and safest position for both the individual and society. But the regrettable failure of the Eighteenth Amendment has demonstrated the fact that the majority of the people of this country are not yet ready for total abstinence, at least when it is attempted through legal coercion. The next best thing—many people think it a better thing—is temperance. Therefore, as I sought to support total abstinence when its achievement seemed possible, so now, and with equal vigor, I would support temperance.

In the attempt to bring about total abstinence through prohibition, an evil even greater than intemperance resulted—namely, a nation-wide disregard for law, with all the attendant abuses that followed in its train. That this intolerable situation should be done away with has seemed to me even more important for the moment than the promotion of temperance. It was for that reason that I took a position more than a year ago in favor of the repeal of the Eighteenth Amendment.

But with repeal the problem is far from solved. As Senator Capper has aptly said, "We may repeal Prohibition, but we cannot repeal the Liquor Problem." If carefully laid plans of control are not made, the old evils against which prohibition was invoked can easily return. Some months ago I came to the conclusion that as a step toward such control, a study of the practice and experience of other countries would be of genuine service. The liquor problem is a world-wide problem and has been wrestled with by many nations. A program of action based on intimate knowledge of their successes and failures, as well as on experience in this country, appeared to me to be a contribution to the thinking of the American people on this subject which might be welcomed. I therefore asked Mr. Raymond B. Fosdick and Mr. Albert L. Scott to organize such a study, which is here offered to the public.

Mr. Fosdick is a practicing attorney, who has made outstanding researches in police and other social problems. Mr. Scott is a practicing engineer, who has also devoted much time and thought to the intensive study of social and religious movements. It seemed to me that this combined professional background would make possible a thorough and well-balanced survey and appraisal of the lessons of experience. Except to ask Mr. Fosdick and Mr. Scott to make the investigation, I have taken no part in the matter. I have made no suggestions as to methods or findings, nor was I acquainted with the conclusions of the authors until the completed manuscript was presented to me. The volume as I read it represents a careful and conscientious investigation; its objectives coincide completely with my own views. Rightly, the first objective is the abolition of lawlessness. Any program offered in lieu of the Eighteenth Amendment must make that its chief aim, even if—and I weigh carefully what I say—the immediate result is temporarily away from temperance.

The second objective is the focusing of all the forces of society upon the development of self-control and temperance as regards the use of alcoholic beverages. As the report aptly says, public standards as a basis for law can be improved only as private standards are improved. To develop the habit of temperance in individuals, to take up again the slow march of education—this is the real and fundamental approach to the problem of alcohol.

The report regards liquor taxation, as it should be regarded, primarily as a helpful factor in forwarding these objectives, and only incidentally as a means of producing income.

I am also greatly impressed with certain principles in the report, which seem to me of profound importance in any present or future effort to deal with the liquor problem. One of them is that law must always be the articulate organ of the desires of living men. Men cannot be made good by force. In the end, intelligent lawmaking rests on the knowledge or estimate of what will be obeyed. Law does not enforce itself. The Eighteenth Amendment embodied an ideal, but it could succeed only with the support of public opinion. The mistake involved in its passage was the failure to foresee that unhappily it might not always have that support.

Another principle which the report develops is that only as the profit motive is eliminated is there any hope of controlling the liquor traffic in the interest of a decent society. To approach the problem from any other angle is only to tinker with it and to insure failure. This point cannot be too heavily stressed.

But the report speaks for itself; it needs no interpretation from me. Two things only would I add: The first is that my confidence in the open-mindedness and sound judgment of the gentlemen who have prepared this report is such that I have no hesitation in commending it to the careful consideration of the American people. The second is that I find myself in complete agreement with the recommendations contained in the report and endorse them fully and unreservedly.

PREFACE

THIS STUDY, INITIATED IN FEBRUARY, 1933, IS BASED PRIMARILY ON FIELD investigation conducted by the members of our staff in England, France, Germany, Italy, Russia, Poland, Finland, Sweden, Norway, and Denmark, as well as in all the Canadian provinces. In addition, extensive examination was made of American experience both under prohibition and in the various states prior to prohibition. We have also analyzed current state legislation which in the last few months has anticipated the repeal of the Eighteenth Amendment. In order to obtain the opinion of representative groups as to what measure and plan of liquor control were feasible in the various states, members of the staff have interviewed many people in different parts of the country—judges, lawyers, clergymen, social workers, newspaper editors, representatives of the Foreign Language Information Service, distillers, brewers, members of the Federal Bureau of Industrial Alcohol and the Prohibition Bureau, law enforcement officers, police officials, college presidents, members of the state boards of control already established, and others. A representative cross-section of American opinion, as geographically widespread as the time permitted, was thus obtained.

It has been our purpose not only to outline broad general principles but to point the way to methods of liquor control supported by the best opinion and experience which we could secure both in this country and abroad.

Many people have helped in this study, and it is impossible to mention by name all those to whom our thanks are due. But we acknowledge with gratitude the generous measure of time and patience, as well as the uniform and unwearied courtesy and helpfulness which all of us engaged in this under taking encountered both here and abroad.

Particular reference is due those most closely associated with us. Their devoted work and enthusiasm have made this book possible. Indeed, while we assume responsibility for the volume as its authors, it has been the product of group consideration, and to this group we would pay a sincere tribute of thanks. It consisted of the following:

Mr. Leonard V. Harrison, of the Bureau of Social Hygiene, who visited Denmark, Sweden, Norway, Finland, and England, and who, more than any other one person, is responsible for the chapters on the systems of control; Dr. Luther Gulick of Columbia University, Director of the Institute of Public Administration, whose expert knowledge of governmental practices has been of incalculable assistance; Mr. Everett Colby, who studied the situation in Russia and England, and who brought to our subsequent discussions an intimate knowledge of public life; Mr. Chauncey Belknap, whom we have consulted on legal questions; Mr. A. LeRoy Chipman, who spent several months studying the existing control plans in every Canadian province; Dr. Frank A. Ross of Columbia University, who studied particularly the history of liquor control; Mr. Frank B. Amos, who interviewed many prominent Americans, especially in the Middle West and South; Miss Elizabeth Laine, who worked on problems connected with existing legislation; Mr. Joseph F. Shadgen, who contributed generously from his store of knowledge of the actual business of manufacturing alcoholic beverages; Dr. Theodore Abel of Columbia University, who carried on a study in Poland, Germany, and Austria; Dr. Vittorio Racca of the Institute of Human Relations at Yale University, who surveyed the liquor control system of Italy; Mrs. Margaret Grant Schneider, who interviewed representatives of many groups, assisted in research work, and carried a heavy load of office detail; and Mr. Alexander L. Radomski, who served as a research worker in source material.

This study is the result of their labors, and whatever is creditable in the report is due to them.

Raymond B. Fosdick
Albert L. Scott

49 West 49 Street
New York City,
October 2, 1933

TOWARD LIQUOR CONTROL

Chapter One

THE BACKGROUND OF THE PROBLEM

THE ATTEMPT TO CONTROL BY LAW THE USE OF INTOXICATING BEVERAGES IS many centuries old. In America legal restrictions surrounded the sale of liquor from the earliest Colonial days. Temperance movements have come and gone; organized efforts for moderation, backed by moral suasion, have had their day; but in all the long struggle with one of the most difficult human problems law has remained our chief weapon in trying to curb the social consequences of excess.

Liquor legislation in America presents a bewildering picture of shifting public sentiment and vacillating policies. The pendulum has swung from one extreme to another; reaction from a particular experiment repeatedly has carried succeeding legislation far in the opposite direction. Laws have been hastily and immaturely conceived, and new experiment have been cramped by minute legislative restrictions and handed over to the tender mercies of the spoils system, making success under any circumstances impossible. There are but few instances in America in which scientific consideration or long and patient study by experts has been given to the ends desired, the issues at stake or the principles involved. Makeshift and improvisation have far too often been the tools employed. Public irritation and impatience have greeted the progress of each new system of control and, frequently, before the system has had an opportunity to prove itself one way or the other a new system has been devised and put into operation. In four different periods in her history Iowa had some form of state-wide prohibition, alternating with license systems of one type or another. Rhode Island swung from license to prohibition and back again three times in less than forty years.

1

A century of liquor legislation in Massachusetts can be broken up into the following approximate periods: twelve years of stringent license, eight years of qualified prohibition, sixteen years of the so called "Main type" of prohibition, one year of high license with local option, a six-year return to modified prohibition, thirteen years of low license, eighteen years of high license, twelve years of high license with local option, and finally prohibition.

It will be noticed that prohibition itself is by no means a new idea. Many states experimented with it before 1920. Between 1846 and 1855, thirteen states—more than one-third of those that then existed—adopted it in one form or another, including New York, Illinois, Massachusetts and Rhode Island. Its fortunes varied from a trial of one year in New York and two years in Illinois, Delaware and Iowa to forty-eight years in New Hampshire, fifty in Vermont and seventy in Maine, in the last state with a two-year break. By 1863 the thirteen prohibition states had shrunk to six, and, of these six, five recanted later.

A second wave of state-wide prohibition, which began during the 1880's, represented, in part at least, the return to dry status of those states in which this experiment had previously been tried and discarded. Altogether eight states were enrolled under the prohibition flag during this period, of which five later withdrew. By 1904 only three remained.

A third wave, essentially Southern and Western, developed at the end of the first decade of the Twentieth Century. When we entered the war in 1917, 25 states had prohibition laws, and the foundations of the Eighteenth Amendment had been definitely laid. By 1919, prior to the adoption of the Amendment, the number had risen to 33. In this list were three states in which prohibition had been in continuous operation for years, and six others which had experimented with this type of control on earlier occasions.[1]

The same kind of kaleidoscopic change characterized the em-

---

[1] The thirty-three prohibition states in 1919, prior to the adoption of the Amendment, comprised approximately 80 per cent of the area of the United States and 52 per cent of the population. If dry local option areas in non-prohibition states are included, the total dry area at this time comprised 95 per cent of the country and involved 68 per cent of the population.

ployment of the license system. At one time or another in the various states—and often in muddled relationship—every kind of licensing device and expedient has been attempted: high license fees, low license fees, segregation of licenses in relation to residences, schools and churches or restriction in fixed ratios to population, and an almost limitless variety of classifications of licenses. The county dispensary method has also been tried; indeed, during the last decade of the Nineteenth Century and the first few years of the Twentieth, it made rapid headway, particularly in the South, only to be overwhelmed by the third tidal wave of the prohibition movement. Similarly, South Carolina for fourteen years carried on a limited and unsatisfactory experiment with the state dispensary system. South Dakota for two years had legislation providing for such a system, but no dispensaries were actually established.

Not only have the policies themselves been subject to rapidly shifting changes but the methods of administration as well. Checks and balances and ingeniously conceived restrictions, state excise boards, county excise boards, municipal excise boards, judicial boards, local option plans or confused combinations of several administrative ideas and principles—all these have been the product of uncertain and bewildered legislatures, harassed into believing that somewhere or in some fashion there could be found or developed a legal device which would completely solve, once and for all, the problems of the liquor trade. It was this search for a cure-all that brought us the Eighteenth Amendment. Here at last was a magic formula, a simple solution, by which, in relation to more than 100,000,000 people, age-old evils could with one stroke be eliminated.

After fourteen years the American people have renounced this faith. A new amendment, the Twenty-first, repeals the Eighteenth. With apprehension as well as relief the public asks: What shall replace national prohibition?

The Limitations of Law

One can scarcely study the history of liquor legislation leading up to the adoption of the Prohibition Amendment of 1920 without coming to the conclusion that too often we have attempted to impose on law a burden which law by itself is not equipped to carry. We have resorted to law to make up the deficiencies of other agencies of social control. We have tried to govern too largely by means of law tendencies which in their nature do not easily admit of objective treatment and external coercion. We have labored under a belief that law could be used as a short cut to a desired end and that the agencies through which moral objectives are normally sought—for example, the home, the school, the church—could be subordinated to a speedier process. "Nothing is more attractive to the benevolent vanity of men," said James Coolidge Carter, "than the notion that they can effect great improvement in society by the simple process of forbidding all wrong conduct, or conduct that they think is wrong, by law, and of enjoining all good conduct by the same means."

This easy fallacy has marked the evolution of liquor legislation in America. In a delicate field, involving divergent standards and appetites, our main approach has been by way of the police. We have not hesitated to bring habits and customs, widely practiced and widely regarded as innocent, within the scope of our criminal laws. Legislation has seemed to us to contain some redemptive element within itself—as if words on a statute book could by some alchemy alter the tastes and preferences of men. On no other theory can be based an explanation of the intricate legal patchwork which has constituted our chief defense against the abuse of alcohol—one frantic bit of legislation after another in an attempt to minimize and check the evils of overindulgence.

With the passing of the national prohibition experiment there seems to be developing a recognition of the fact that law is not a royal road to a moral goal. We do not wish to underestimate the part that legislation can play as a social function. It cannot by itself set new standards, yet it need not be merely "the culmination of settled habits and customs." It can be a wise blend of accepted principle and courageous experiment, a judicious balance between the tradition and experience of the past and the adventure and promise of the future. But always it must be the articulate organ of the desires of living men. Permanent advance in human society cannot be brought about by night-sticks and patrol wagons. Men cannot be made good by force. The mechanism of society is a matter of stresses and strains in which a large number of factors carry their share of the weight. The lawmaker, if he is wise, will determine how far legal processes are adapted to the ends he seeks to secure. He will learn not to expect too much of the law and he will resist the temptation habitually to convert into legal crimes practices which he deems mischievous or unethical.

In the end intelligent lawmaking rests on the knowledge or estimate of what will be obeyed. Our traditional belief in the efficacy of law as a means of social control resulted in hundreds of liquor statutes which were unenforced and largely unenforceable, either because they did not represent public opinion or because the public opinion they did represent was not sufficiently preponderant in the community. Law does not enforce itself. Its machinery must be set in motion and kept in motion by individual human beings. As Dean Pound of Harvard has pointed out, there must be something more than the abstract content of the legal precept to move human beings to act. Certainly the only standard which the law has any hope of enforcing is the standard prevailing in the community as a whole and not that which prevails in a single group, no matter how enlightened it may be.

In brief, to use the blunt phrase of "Golden Rule" Jones, former Mayor of Toledo: "Law in America is what the people will back up." Its authority is social acquiescence. Its life is in its enforcement. Victorious upon paper, it is powerless elsewhere. The test of its validity is the strength of the social reaction which supports it. Only as it expresses the composite will is it effective in coercing the individual. "The law is only a memorandum," said Emerson. "We are superstitious and esteem the statute somewhat; so much life as it has in the character of living men is its force."

It is obvious that public standards as a basis for law can be improved only as private standards are improved. To develop the habit of temperance in individuals, to take up again the slow march of education—this is the real and fundamental approach to the problem of alcohol. To this point we return again in a later chapter. We raise it at this time because, while we shall deal almost exclusively with legislative arrangements and legal restrictions—and that, indeed, is the primary purpose of this book—we wish at the outset to disavow for ourselves the naïve belief, apparently obtaining in many quarters, that law is the chief bulwark of temperance. In respect to the use of intoxicants, law has its place in registering the requirements of the community with a view to protecting the public order. Of far greater significance, however, in our opinion, are those other agencies of social control, centering in the strengthening of the character of the individual, which touch the roots of the problem as law cannot hope to touch them.

What is the Community?

We have said that no system of liquor control can be successful which does not command the approval of the community. But what is the community which the legislator must have in mind? And how is its opinion on the subject of liquor control to be ascertained? These are problems which for years have tested the ingenuity of students of government. The difficulties are not peculiar to liquor legislation, though there is probably no field of legislation in which mistakes of judgment on these points are more fatal to successful law enforcement.

It was often argued, in justification of the Eighteenth Amendment, that at the time of its adoption an overwhelming percentage of the territory of the United States, and of its population, was under local prohibition laws. But it was a mistake to regard the United States as a single community in which a uniform policy of liquor control could be enforced. When the citizens of the United States wrote prohibition into the Federal Constitution they forgot that this nation is not a social unit with uniform ideas and habits. They overlooked the fact that in a country as large as this, racially diversified, heterogeneous in most aspects of its life and comprising a patchwork of urban and rural areas, no common rule of conduct in regard to a powerful human appetite could possibly be enforced.

The country made another miscalculation, perhaps even more fundamental. It established a system under which the broad matter of policy was settled by the Federal Constitution and by federal law; but the enforcement of that policy was left almost entirely to the police officers and the inferior courts of the local units of government, in the hands of men who were responsible not to the federal government nor to the state government, but to the local voters. Indeed, unless we had been prepared, as we obviously were not, to create a far greater army of federal police agents than were actually marshaled together, no other course was open to us. But it was the centralizing of the determination of policy combined with the decentralizing of the execution of policy that nullified the experiment in those areas where sympathy for its purposes was nonexistent, and brought the inevitable trail of consequences in terms of the bootlegger, hypocrisy, corruption and failure.

With the repeal of the Eighteenth Amendment, therefore, we must assume that the single state becomes the largest community for the legislator to consider. It is safe to say that the country is not at this moment prepared for another enabling constitutional amendment and another federal experiment. We have returned to the individual state the power to deal with the question, and there is no reason to believe that this policy will be reversed—at least for some years to come.

Is even the state too large a community to be subject to a single and uniform policy throughout its length and breadth? The answer to this question must depend upon the size of each commonwealth and the diversity of origin, occupation and interest of its population. There may be some states which for the purpose of liquor legislation constitute single units with a relatively homogeneous population having substantially common origins and social habits. In such states a single liquor policy might safely be applied. On the other hand, there are states which contain both large cities and extensive rural districts. It is hardly necessary to point out that such states are not, for purposes of liquor legislation, single communities. A policy satisfactory to the farming districts in all probability would be too strict for the cities, and even within the limits of a single city there would be subdivisions, the wishes and preferences of which should merit consideration.

It is here that we must fall back upon the principle of "local option," a principle which is in accord with American legislative tradition and undoubtedly offers the most promising measure of success. It places behind all the local officials who administer the system the same public opinion that determines the system. That this principal has its difficulties is patent to anyone who is familiar with the experience of the past, and we shall speak of them in later chapters. The point we would stress at this time is the necessity of bringing the determination of how the liquor problem shall be handled as close as possible to the individual and his home. If conditions in the locality in which he lives are of his own choosing, and if he can reasonably be protected in the maintenance of those conditions, even though the whole system may not be ideal — and certainly it will lack in uniformity — the total result will be more satisfactory than would be an ambitious plan of greater geographical magnitude under which the wishes of thousands of neighborhoods are disregarded in the interest of some shadowy common good.

What does the Community want?

In the violent reaction against the Eighteenth Amendment, what is it that the public has in mind? What principles lie behind this rebellion and what are the objectives that are sought? Fourteen years ago the Prohibition Amendment was adopted with a degree of enthusiasm that surprised even its friends. Today it is summarily rejected. What has caused this swing of the pendulum and what are the motives that have guided it?

The difficulty of finding an answer to these questions is at once apparent. There is no well-defined community of public opinion on this matter. There are varying principals and divergent objectives, and they are not infrequently confused and contradictory, not only as between different sections of the country, but as between different groups and individuals in the same section. Nevertheless, it is perhaps possible to discover in any public question a certain common denominator of belief, a residue of ideas around which opinion centers, not with entire unanimity, to be sure, but with such a reasonable degree of unanimity as to justify the impression of a definite point of view and a well-defined basis for action.

We have been at pains to secure, as far as we could, a cross-section of opinion from all types of leaders of thought and activity in the United States on the subject of liquor control: newspaper editors, political leaders, social workers, clergymen, educators, manufacturers, labor leaders, farmers, businessmen, liquor producers, prohibitionists, government officers now and formerly concerned with the problem of liquor supervision, and others. Over four hundred such leaders were personally interviewed. What we wanted to obtain, if possible, was a body of principles upon which recommendations for a new type of liquor control could conceivably be based. We wanted an understanding of motives, a knowledge of objectives.

Out of the mass of opinions obtained it is possible to set down a few definite principles behind which, it can be said with reasonable accuracy, a substantial degree of public support exists. We have adopted these principles as our own and they have served as guides in the writing of this volume and in the preparation of our recommendations. Briefly, they are as follows:

1. At all costs—even if it means a temporary increase in consumption of alcohol—bootlegging, racketeering and the whole wretched nexus of crime that developed while the Eighteenth Amendment was in force must be wiped out. The defiance of law that has grown up in the last fourteen years, the hypocrisy, the breakdown of governmental machinery, the demoralization in public and private life, is a stain on America that can no longer be tolerated. The American people are definitely aroused in a determination to clean up this source of corruption and to reëstablish the integrity and dignity of the law.

2. Wide areas of the public are unconvinced that the use of al-

coholic beverages is in itself reprehensible. That there is grave peril of immoderate use is unanimously conceded. In respect to every human desire, intemperance has always been the chief frailty of mankind. But while hundreds of thousands of people are by preference and practice teetotalers, public opinion will not support the thesis that the temperate use of alcohol is inconsistent with sobriety, self-control, good citizenship and social responsibility. More than that, many people believe that such moderate use can be made an agreeable phase of a civilized mode of living.

3. The saloon, as it existed in pre-prohibition days, was a menace to society and must never be allowed to return. Behind its blinds degradation and crime were fostered, and under its principle of stimulated sales poverty and drunkenness, big profits and political graft, found a secure foothold. Public opinion has not forgotten the evils symbolized by this disreputable institution and it does not intend that it shall worm its way back into our social life.

4. Despite the reaction from the Eighteenth Amendment, America is in no mood to stand any aggressiveness on the part of the brewers, the distillers and the liquor trade generally. The memory of their campaigns against temperance, of their corrupt legislative activities and of their insolent intrusion into our political life in the days before prohibition, is still alive. Any indication that they are once more pushing their business in violation of decent social standards will bring the pendulum swinging back.

5. Public opinion is gratified by the record of sobriety that has attended the return of beer. It is distinctly apprehensive over the prospective legalized return of spirits. For America aspires to be a temperate nation. It has a passionate desire that its young people shall be protected against the greedy commercialization of the liquor trade and the pitfalls of intemperance. It dreads the hazards and inefficiencies that attend immoderation. It is fully prepared to take drastic steps if, as a result of the present attitude of toleration, conditions should once more get out of control.

6. America is inclined to believe that there is some definite solution for the liquor problem—some method other than bone-dry

prohibition—that will allow a sane and moderate use of alcohol to those who desire it, and at the same time minimize the evils of excess. There is no unanimity of opinion as to what that solution shall be, but the people at the moment are in an adventurous mood. A new philosophy of change is in the air, and political ideas are now being put into effect which were unthinkable even a decade ago. The question is asked: Why should we follow the old pre-prohibition route? Why is it not possible to strike out on a fresh trail? If in relation to every other business new social and political controls are daily being devised, why in relation to this liquor business should we not create a new technique, a new method, by which it can be brought within the compass of what the public really desires?

The Conclusions of this Report

This report attempts to find an answer to this type of question, and our conclusions may be briefly summarized as follows:

1. State-wide, bone-dry prohibition will prove unsuccessful in controlling the problem of alcohol, unless such a system has behind it overwhelming public support. Even then it will tend to carry in its trail the hypocrisy and lawlessness which marked the national experiment.

2. The experience of every country supports the idea that light wines and beers do not constitute a serious social problem.

3. While many states will doubtless follow the license method in the control of beverages of higher alcoholic content, this method contains a fundamental flaw in that it retains the private profit motive which makes inevitable the stimulation of sales.

4. Wide experience in many countries indicates that the best approach to the problem of heavier alcoholic beverages is through state control. By state control we mean specifically a system by which the state, through a central authority, maintains an exclusive monopoly of retail sale for off-premises consumption. This authority determines prices, fixes the location of its stores, controls advertising, and in general manages the trade in such a way as to meet a minimum, unstimulated demand within conditions established solely in the interests of society.

5. The primary objective of taxation should be social control, not revenue. Taxes should be levied not with the idea of filling the public treasury at whatever cost to public morality and efficiency, but as a method of reducing the consumption of alcohol.

6. Education in its broadest sense has a greater part to play in creating a sober nation than has legislative enactment. Temperance lies in the character, standards and self-discipline of individual men and women. Education is a slow process, but it carries a heavier share of the burden of social control than does legal coercion.

Chapter Two

THE LEGACY OF PROHIBITION

THE ADOPTION OF THE TWENTY-FIRST AMENDMENT DOES NOT, AS MANY people think, wipe the slate clean for completely new systems of liquor control. It leaves untouched he laws of constitutional provisions now existing in the various states. Moreover, a number of federal statutes relating to liquor were passed before the adoption of the Eighteenth Amendment and have never been repealed. After a period of more or less suspended animation, these laws now revive and may become potent instruments of control. Before discussing the new legislation proposed in this report, we must, therefore, pause to examine briefly the background of existing law against which our recommendations are projected.

The Twenty-first Amendment, aside from procedural matter, contains two clauses: the first repeals the Eighteenth Amendment; the second forbids the transportation of intoxicants into any state for delivery or use in violation of the laws of that state.[1] Consequently, prohibition, in so far as it is established in state laws or state constitutions, will not be eradicated by the adoption of the new Amendment. Instead, the power of a dry state to exclude liquor shipments, previously protected only by Act of Congress,[2] will be given the added sanction of an express constitutional guarantee. No change hereafter in the temper of Congress can deprive dry states of the right to stop liquor shipments at their borders, a right which received its first statutory recognition only twenty years ago.

---

[1] For the text of the Amendment, see Appendix I.
[2] The Webb-Kenyon Act of March 1, 1913 (c. 90, 37 Stat. 699); see also the Reed Amendment (Act March 3, 1917, c. 162, 39 Stat. 1069) and the Wilson Original Packages Act of Aug. 8, 1890 (c. 728, 26 Stat. 313). For the text of these acts see Appendix I.

In spite of the adoption of the Twenty-first Amendment, prohibition will continue to operate in over half the states, thirty in number.[3] In almost one-third, fourteen in number,[4] resort must be had to the difficult process of modifying the state constitution before the sale of alcoholic beverages can be legalized. It is true that there has been a marked trend away from state prohibition. Since January 1, 1932, five states have repealed the dry clauses in their state constitutions and five others have rescinded their prohibition statutes. In eight others constitutional referenda are scheduled during 1933 and 1934. But it is safe to say that procedural obstacles standing in the way of a change will be enough to keep some states legally dry for many months after the passage of the Twenty-first Amendment.

State-wide Prohibition

Nation-wide prohibition has been pronounced a failure. The task was too complex and required too rapid a shift of custom and habit to succeed in a land as extensive, as populous, and as heterogeneous as ours. It does not follow, however, that prohibition in smaller units is necessarily headed for the same complete failure. As a matter of fact, the history of prohibition legislation in the several states prior to 1919 indicates that under the right circumstances it may achieve some degree of success in making intoxicants difficult to obtain, thereby removing temptation from the young and from persons disposed to alcoholic excesses. As has been stated, three of our states found it a sufficiently good principle to govern their policies for many decades.

It should be realized, although it seldom is, that prohibition is not a simple or single concept. Under the laws of the different states it has appeared in a multiplicity of forms, varying from practically complete non-sale to minimized restriction on sale. Seldom, if ever, has all use of alcoholic beverages been prohibited. Even the legis-

---

[3] Alabama, Arkansas, Florida, Georgia, Idaho, Iowa, Kansas, Kentucky, Maine, Michigan, Minnesota, Mississippi, Missouri, Nebraska, New Hampshire, North Carolina, North Dakota, Ohio, Oklahoma, Oregon, Pennsylvania, South Carolina, South Dakota, Tennessee, Texas, Utah, Vermont, Virginia, West Virginia and Wyoming.

[4] Florida, Idaho, Kansas, Kentucky, Maine, Nebraska, Ohio, Oklahoma, Oregon, South Dakota, Texas, Utah, West Virginia and Wyoming.

lative acts generally restricting manufacture, sale or transportation have ordinarily contained exceptions. Thus, legislators have rarely attempted to prohibit manufacture of wines, beers and ciders in the home. Indeed, commercial manufacture and sale of the lighter beverages have sometimes been permitted. Under all but the dryest laws sale has been licensed for medicinal purposes. Many dry states have allowed importation by the package from outside, and there are plenty of other instances of modifications of the prohibition principle which were employed prior to the Eighteenth Amendment in an effort to meet particular demands.

The possible future success of state-wide prohibition will depend entirely upon whether there is within the state an overwhelming majority in favor of this type of control. On no other basis can it hope to be even moderately successful. Any law relating to liquor has a broad incidence; it touches many people directly. Consequently, its popular backing must be strong. If an uncompromising, bone-dry prohibition is attempted, failure to marshal a preponderant sentiment behind it will, we believe, admit all the abuses which have recently been experienced under the national régime. Each state is familiar with the peculiar manifestations of these abuses within its borders. Undoubtedly federal repeal has altered some of the conditions, and it is possible that in a few states factors favorable to the retention of prohibition are discernible. As a general rule, however, it would seem to be advisable for a state to adhere to prohibition only when there is tangible evidence that public opinion is running definitely and irresistibly in its favor. No other method of handling the liquor problem depends so completely upon undeviating public support.

Even in a state where a large majority of the voters have expressed themselves in favor of a thoroughgoing non-sale policy it may be eminently desirable to make concessions to an irreconcilable minority as a means of eliminating an organized bootlegging traffic. Legalized importation by package for personal use has been one of the methods by which some so called prohibition states in the past have secured respect for the law. Whether or not this modification or some other is advisable, a state that retains prohibition will, if it is wise, adapt its statute to what it can reasonably enforce. Nothing is to be gained by passing a law which serves merely to satisfy the consciences of those responsible for it.

Before 1919 it was often contended that the wet states failed in their responsibility to adjoining dry states, and there was much to support the charge. The outlook at present, as we have said, is for a reduction of the field occupied by state-wide prohibition. If in the end a few dry strongholds remain, they should not forget that they also have a responsibility to the states in which intoxicants are legally obtainable. Unless past experience is reversed, such surviving dry areas will become a paradise for bootleggers. Operating from there as a base, the illicit traffic should not be allowed to run cheap, inferior liquor into the neighboring wet states for sale in competition with the legal, but perhaps higher priced, article. Anyone who regards this as an illusory danger will do well to examine the efforts of the Canadian provincial governments to prevent invasion by American bootleggers selling tax-free liquor.

State Prohibition in the Past

In view of the widespread evils which followed the adoption of the Eighteenth Amendment, we frankly are not impressed with the possibilities of prohibition as a method of control, even in individual states. We believe in stringent regulation of beverages of high alcoholic content. We do not believe that such regulation is possible under a strict form of prohibition. Moreover, the by-products of prohibition in terms of law defiance represent, in our opinion, too great a price to pay for whatever gains may be secured. These by-products have not appeared for the first time as a result of the national experiment. They were present in connection with dry states long before 1919.

In 1903 the Committee of Fifty, under the leadership of such men as President Eliot of Harvard, Seth Low, Dr. Francis G. Peabody and others, published a summary of the results of ten-year survey of the liquor problem. Their comments on the operation of the prohibition in two states, Maine and Iowa, where it had long been tried, are pertinent even today. After giving full credit to the accomplishments of prohibition in making intoxicants difficult to obtain, the report continues:

> But prohibitory legislation has failed to exclude intoxicants completely even from districts where public sentiment has been favorable. In districts where public sentiment has been adverse or strongly divided, the traffic in alcoholic beverages has been sometimes repressed or harassed, but never exterminated or rendered unprofitable. In Maine and Iowa there have always been counties and municipalities in complete and successful rebellion against law....Prohibition has, of course, failed to subdue the drinking passion, which will forever prompt resistance to all restrictive legislation.
>
> There have been concomitant evils of prohibitory legislation. The efforts to enforce it during forty years past have had some unlooked-for effects on public respect for courts, judicial procedure, oaths, and law in general, and for officers of the law, legislators, and public servants. The public have seen law defied, a whole generation of habitual law-breakers schooled in evasion and shamelessness, courts ineffective through fluctuations of policy, delays, perjuries, negligences, and other miscarriages of justice, officers of the law double-faced and mercenary, legislators timid and insincere, candidates for office hypocritical and truckling, and office-holders unfaithful to pledges and to reasonable public expectation.... The liquor traffic, being very profitable, has been able, when attacked by prohibitory legislation, to pay fines, bribes, hush-money, and assessments for political purposes to large amounts. This money has tended to corrupt the lower courts, the police administration, political organizations, and even the electorate itself. Wherever the voting force of the liquor traffic and its allies is considerable, candidates for office and office-holders are tempted to serve a dangerous trade interest which is often in antagonism to the public interest. Frequent yielding to this temptation causes general degeneration in public life, breeds contempt for the public service, and of course, makes the service less desirable for upright men. Again, the sight of justices, constables, and informers enforcing a prohibitory law far enough to get from it the fines and fees which profit them, but not far enough to extinguish the traffic and so cut off the source of their profits, is demoralizing to society at large. All legislation intended to put restrictions on the liquor traffic, except perhaps the simple tax, is more or less liable to these objections; but the prohibitory legislation is the worst of all in these respects, because it stimulates to the utmost the resistance of the liquor-dealers and their supporters.[5]

---

[5] The Committee of Fifty, *The Liquor Problem*, pp. 50-53.

This was written more than a quarter of a century ago, but it can be read with profit by those who still think of unqualified, bone-dry prohibition as the simplest and most effective method of handling the problem of alcohol.

Chapter Three

LIGHT WINES AND BEERS VS. SPIRITS

WE COME NOW TO THE SITUATION EXISTING IN THOSE STATES IN WHICH, BY the repeal of the Eighteenth Amendment, the slate has been wiped clean for a new experiment in liquor control. What is the road to be taken? From what point do we see the beginning of a path toward temperance?

American liquor legislation in the past has, as we have seen, been guided more by emotion than by reason or experience. In the stumbling search for a law to cure the drink evil, legislators seldom paused to inquire what drinks should be the main target of attack. To many earnest and sincere temperance workers alcohol in any form was a vice. Beer containing 3.2 per cent of alcohol was condemned indiscriminately along with whiskey having a content of 30 to 45 per cent.[1] In most states, under the old régime, a single license permitted the sale of both beer and whiskey. As a result, they were commonly sold over the same counter, and often the chief source of profit of the "beer saloon" was its sales of hard liquor.

True to this American tradition of treating all alcoholic beverages alike, the Volstead Act defined as "intoxicating liquor" any beverage containing one-half of one per cent, or more, of alcohol by volume. An overwhelming weight of medical and scientific testimony to the contrary was brushed aside by Congress. Facts were not wanted when they were in conflict with the fervently held belief that alcohol in a concentration of one-half of one per cent, or more, makes a drink unfit for human consumption.

---

[1] Unless otherwise stated, the basis of measurement used in this book is by weight rather than by volume.

What is an Intoxicating Beverage?

A rational approach to the problem of liquor control requires an about-face and a new viewpoint. We should start by inquiring what concentration of alcohol makes a beverage intoxicating in fact to the ordinary man. When the alcoholic content is below that point, a drink should be subject to little, if any, restraint upon its use. The sale of stronger drinks should be regulated under a program which, so far as is practicable, discourages consumption with increasing strictness as the alcoholic content increases. Such a system directs its spear-head against alcohol in the forms most liable to abuse by man, and, by permitting relative freedom in the use of the weaker drinks, tends to promote temperance.

Where shall the lines be drawn in setting up such a plan of control? A natural and convenient division is between fermented beverages and distilled liquors. The fermented drinks, consisting mainly of beers and wines, have a range in alcoholic content up to 12 per cent. Distilled liquors, which include whiskey and gin, usually contain from 30 to 45 per cent of alcohol.[2]

The distilled liquors are thus seen to be in a class by themselves, with an alcoholic strength far in excess of wines and beers. This difference should be made the basis of a radical difference in treatment under the law. It is true that even the heaviest spirits may be consumed in such moderation as to avoid injurious consequences and that it is possible to over indulge in wine or beer. But the experience and common sense of mankind have always recognized the difference between the two—if legislators have not.

No one will deny that whiskey and gin are more intoxicating than beer and wine. The argument for treating the two classes of beverages alike in the past has been that the beer drinker of today becomes the whiskey sot of tomorrow. There may be danger that this will occur if 3.2 per cent beer can be sold only over the same bar and subject to the same conditions as whiskey. Since there is a greater profit in whiskey, the bartender is under a constant temptation to push its sale. But we find no definite evidence to support the

---

[2] For a tabulation of the alcoholic strength of various beverages, see Appendix V.

theory that satisfying a taste for beer develops a craving for whiskey. On the contrary, we believe that if beers and wines are more easily obtainable than distilled liquors, and are sold in different places and under different conditions, there is a reasonable ground to expect that the taste of those who wish to drink will be diverted to the lighter and less harmful beverages.

3.2 per cent Beer as a non-intoxicating Beverage

Every consideration of social control suggests the frank acceptance and treatment of beer containing not more than 3.2 per cent of alcohol as a non-intoxicating beverage. While this line may not be drawn with strict scientific accuracy, it has been popularly accepted as a result of the Act of Congress of March 22, 1933, permitting the sale of 3.2 per cent beer. Since that date the nation has been a laboratory in which a remarkable experiment has been tried. During this time such beer was sold, even in populous centers like New York City, with little restraint. For some weeks it was obtainable like ice cream at any soda fountain. It has been drunk in enormous quantities. Yet the testimony is almost unanimous that there has been no increase in drunkenness, no disorder, no increased resort to illicit hard liquor. The evidence, as we have found it, is all the other way. Bootleggers have lost part of their patronage; in some places arrests for drunkenness have positively declined.

The continued, unrestricted sale of beer having an alcoholic content of not more than 3.2 per cent is clearly the part of wisdom. Such beer should be obtainable by the bottle, for off-premises consumption, practically without limitation. Its sale should be allowed by grocery stores, drug stores, delicatessen and general stores, and indeed by any merchant who so desires. A vendor's permit should be required, but the cost should be low and there should be no restriction on the number of such permits. The sale of such beer by the glass, with or without meals, should be permitted in restaurants, hotels, beer gardens, clubs and, indeed, in any reputable establishment.

The Control of Natural Wines

Wines naturally fermented—not in excess of, say, 10 to 12 per cent—should be sold by the bottle for off-premises consumption as freely as 3.2 per cent beer.[3] But as compared with 3.2 per cent beer, a greater measure of restriction should govern the sale of wine for on-premises consumption. Natural wine should be sold by the glass only with meals. It follows that the sale of wine for on-premises consumption should be restricted to bona fide restaurants, dining rooms and clubs.

In summary, we recommend that the following classification of permits for the sale of 3.2 per cent beer and of wines be adopted:

A. Permits to sell 3.2 per cent beer and naturally fermented wines not in excess of 10 to 12 per cent by the bottle for off-premises consumption.
B. Permits to sell 3.2 per cent beer for on-premises consumption with or without meals.
C. Permits for sale of 3.2 per cent beer and natural wines at hotels, restaurants or clubs for consumption on the premises with meals.

The sale of heavier beers, fortified wines and spirits will be discussed in the following chapters.

•   •   •   •   •

To many people this liberal policy in relation to the control of beers and wines may seem a betrayal of the cause of temperance. With them no compromise with liquor in any form is possible, and the world they desire is a world in which alcoholic beverages are not consumed at all. We have no wish to argue with this point of view. Those who hold it have every right to their conviction and have every right to promulgate their conviction by persuasion and education in the interest of total abstinence, personally chosen and practiced. To write this conviction upon our statute books, however, as an affair of legal coercion, is another matter altogether. Today we are

---

[3] While a 10 to 12 per cent dividing line is more or less arbitrary, it represents the average upper limit of the stronger natural wines.

confronted with practical realities. It is not a question of the kind of world we might prefer; it is a question of what we can achieve in the kind of world we have. It is a question of human tastes and appetites which, as we have discovered, cannot be eliminated by statute. In our opinion there is but one major proposition to be faced in relation to alcohol. Granting that millions of our people will not drink at all, how can the cause of temperance best be served among those who choose to drink? It is because we believe that the whole temperance movement will be materially helped if the sale of beverages of low alcoholic content is liberalized that we have been led to the recommendations contained in this chapter.

Chapter Four

REGULATION BY LICENSE

In dealing with the sale of heavier beers, fortified wines and spirits, we are confronted with a question infinitely vexatious and complex. Indeed, it is the heart of the liquor problem, and for many centuries its attempted solution has brought grief and disillusionment. If light beers and wines were the only alcoholic beverages consumed, the social implications of the liquor trade would present but few difficulties and the task of the legislator would be simple. It is, primarily, the distilled liquors and, secondarily, the heavier beers and wines that create the real problems.

Apart from prohibition, which attempts to meet these problems by bold statutory abolition, there are two main classifications of governmental control: the license method and the public monopoly method. In this chapter we shall explore the possibilities of the license method as a way of handling the stronger alcoholic beverages.

CONTROL BY LICENSE

The licensing of private manufacturers and sellers of alcoholic beverages was the almost universal form of liquor control employed by the United States prior to the advent of prohibition. There were a few outstanding exceptions; notably in New England, in South Carolina, in Athens, Georgia, in Iowa and in South Dakota. Although the basic features of the licensing systems were much the same, there were many variations in respect to constitution of the license-issuing authorities, terms of licenses and fees, number of licensed places in proportion to population, and local option provisions.

24

In the Canadian provinces and in Norway, Sweden and Finland the licensing system has been abandoned in favor of state management, or "monopoly" as it is called. In Russia also a state monopoly system has been created. In Germany private manufacturers of alcohol may sell only to the federal (Reich) monopoly, but blended alcoholic beverages are sold by private traders under local regulations. By and large, around the world, however, the licensing plan is the dominant method of liquor regulation. England and Holland, perhaps, furnish the best examples of licensing systems in countries where people are accustomed to drink a proportionately greater amount of heavier beers and spirits than is consumed in the so-called wine drinking countries.

The License System in England

England has what we believe to be the most successful license system. Although this system has never been displaced by prohibition or, except for the Carlisle plan, by any scheme of government ownership, and although the country has never even experimented with local option, the record for improvement in temperance in England is exceeded by no country except Denmark. Since 1913 consumption of spirits has decreased 60 percent and beer consumption 41 per cent, while convictions for drunkenness have fallen 74 per cent during the same period. Though undoubtedly influenced by the economic depression and by regulations imposed in connection with the dole, this achievement is attributed in part to the policy of reduction in the number of licensed premises, to high excise duties and to reduction in the hours of sale at public houses and at other places where liquor is available for consumption on the premises.[1]

---

[1] Under the English system liquor licenses are issued locally by justices of the peace, who generally serve without compensation. As a means of tax administration, an excise license, issued by the Treasury, is also required. The jurisdiction of the local justices is limited to the county, city or borough for which they are appointed.

Justices' licenses are required for all premises where intoxicating liquor is sold, except retail establishments which sell spirits and wine for consumption off the premises, theaters, a few premises known as the "Ancient Vintners Company" and registered clubs.

Licenses are usually granted for a year, but the justices have discretion to extend the period to a maximum of seven years. The justices also have considerable discretion in the awarding of licenses. They pass on the suitability of the applicant and are obliged to consider objections raised against the granting

The adult education movement in England and the increased interest in sports share, according to many observers, the credit for this remarkable reduction in the consumption of alcohol.

The trend in England is toward the improvement and strengthening of the license system. In 1931 a Royal Commission on Licensing proposed an even more rapid reduction of licenses than that which had been effected to date. Other recommendations of this Commission included: a policy of public house improvement; the creation of special hotel and restaurant licenses to which certain privileges would be attached; and more effective control over the supply of intoxicating liquor in clubs. Perhaps the most significant recommendation in the report looked toward the creation of a National Licensing Commission, as a supplement to the local licensing bodies.

American vs. English Experience

The licensing system has a good name in England, but in most sections of this country prior to 1920 it had a bad name. Before national prohibition, the saloon achieved an evil notoriety. Politics were often bought by the liquor interests; vice and gambling came to be regarded as normal accompaniments of the liquor trade; and the abuse of drink, fostered by the drive for profits, produced its share of poverty and misery. All these evils were bred under the licensing system, and it was the complete breakdown of this system that gave momentum to the national prohibition movement.

Are these abuses inevitable incidents of any licensing régime, or can a system be worked out which affords reasonable hope of repeating the successful English experience? We must remember, of course, that English social and governmental conditions are by no means similar to our own and that a system that works in

---

of a particular license. They must also approve the structural condition of the premises to be licensed.

One outstanding feature of the English system of liquor control is its strict limitation of the hours of sale, a measure adopted during the war under the Defence of the Realm Act. In London, for example, sales are limited to a maximum of nine hours between 11 A.M. and 11 P.M. with a compulsory break of at least two hours in the early afternoon. The licensing justices have the power further to restrict these hours. On Sundays and certain holidays the period of sale is limited to five hours.

one country cannot necessarily be made to work in another. For instance, the high character of the justices of the peace in England, by whom liquor licenses are issued, furnishes a guarantee of continuity of policy and disinterested supervision which cannot easily find a parallel in this country. The English public house is not in local politics, for the reason that nothing could conceivably be gained by such intrusion. The justice of the peace is appointed for life by the Lord Chancellor of the Kingdom and he cannot be "reached" or influenced by threat of defeat at election time.

Again, England has a tradition of public order and respect for law that is sadly lacking in this country. The bootlegger and the gangster are not known there, and the speakeasy has not developed. The British are inclined to accept with good-humored tolerance the increasingly rigid restrictions of the licensing system. Certainly there are no organized attempts to defeat it. With such a background of social habit, a particular system of control might easily succeed in England whereas with us it might soon be undermined.

The fact remains, however, that in America no state legislature has taken full advantage of the possibilities of the license method as an instrument of liquor control. The licensing systems of pre-prohibition days did not deserve the name of system. Ordinarily system was wholly lacking. The law was a hodge-podge of enactment and amendment. It was not the expression of a carefully thought-out plan for social control of the liquor problem, but was usually an ill-considered patchwork resulting from the conflict of interest between liquor dealers and reformers. Seldom was any attempt made to discriminate between the handling of beer and of hard liquor. License administration was frequently in the hands of those who had a personal interest in making control ineffectual.

Suggested Methods of License

Our investigations have convinced us that these weaknesses cannot easily be eradicated from the operation of the license system in America, and, for reasons which we shall later discuss, we recommend the frank abandonment of further legislative tinkering with licenses and the acceptance of an altogether different method of control. At the same time, some states will doubtless be tempted to follow beaten paths and adhere to the old rules. Therefore, our task in preparing this report would be incompletely performed if we failed to present an outline of what we consider the soundest possible licensing system, if such a system must be adopted.

First: The outstanding prerequisite of a licensing system is the creation of a single state licensing board, with state-wide authority and responsibility, appointed by the governor and working through a well-paid, full-time managing director. The administrative personnel of the board should be appointed on a merit basis, free from politics and with a permanent tenure. The board should have an appropriation commensurate with its responsibilities.

It is possible that the state board should be supplemented by local agencies in metropolitan centers and by advisory boards in other areas. In general, however, experience has proved that a licensing board with state-wide powers is more efficient, more responsive to broad public opinion and more free from political influence than autonomous county or municipal bodies can possibly be. The state board should control both beverage and industrial alcohol and should be responsible for the granting and revoking of all licenses. It should also be given the widest possible discretion in regard to the issuance of regulations. Indeed, flexibility of administration within broad limits of policy determined by the legislature is a cardinal principle.

Second: The intelligence, character and integrity of the members of this board are considerations of the first importance. Unless these qualities are conspicuously present, the licensing system will be defeated before it starts. The members should be given long terms of office and should be eligible for reappointment. Their security of tenure will help to make them independent of political pressure. Salaries should be substantial, to attract the best brains obtainable. Under no circumstances should appointments to the board be made on the basis of partisan political considerations.

Nor should resort be had to a bipartisan board in the mistaken belief that this device eliminates politics. In practice, it turns public departments over to the keeping of *both* parties.

Third: The "tied house," and every device calculated to place the retail establishment under obligation to a particular distiller or brewer, should be prevented by all available means. "Tied houses," that is, establishments under contract to sell exclusively the product of one manufacturer, were, in many cases, responsible for the bad name of the saloon. The "tied house" system had all the vices of absentee ownership. The manufacturer knew nothing and cared nothing about the community. All he wanted was increased sales. He saw none of the abuses, and as a non-resident he was beyond local social influence. The "tied house" system also involved a multiplicity of outlets, because each manufacturer had to have a sales agency in a given locality. In this respect the system was not unlike that now used in the sale of gasoline, and with the same result: a large excess of sales outlets. Whether or not this is of concern to the pubic in the case of gasoline, in relation to the liquor problem it is a matter of crucial importance because of its effect in stimulating competition in the retail sale of alcoholic beverages. "Tied houses" should, therefore, be prohibited, and every opportunity for the evasion of this system should, if possible, be foreseen and blocked.[2]

There are many devices used by brewers and distillers to achieve this same end, such as the furnishing of bars, electric signs, refrigerating equipment, the extension of credit, the payment of rebates, the furnishing of warranty bonds when required to guarantee the fulfillment of license conditions and of bail bonds when the dealer is haled into court. A license law should endeavor to prohibit all such relations between the manufacturer and the retailer, difficult though this may be.

---

[2] Almost every beer and general liquor law that has recently been enacted includes this provision, e.g., Rhode Island (Laws 1933, Chapter 2013, Section 48). In some states, as in Illinois (Laws 1933, Page 518, Section 9) and New York (Laws 1933, Chapter 180, Section 86), the manufacturer and the retail licensee are jointly held responsible for any violations of this provision. In Indiana (Laws 1933, Chapter 80, Section 21) and in Iowa (Laws 1933, Chapter 37, Section 26) the gift of equipment such as bars, refrigerators, furniture, electric signs, etc., by manufacturers is expressly prohibited.

Fourth: Suitable restrictions should be established by the license law or by administrative regulation with respect to the number and character of *places* where liquor may be sold. This is regarded as of the highest significance in England, where great effort is being made to reduce the number of licenses from year to year and to improve the appearance and character of licensed places. The number of licenses may be limited on a population basis as is done in Massachusetts and Rhode Island under the new law.[3]

Closely related to the limitation of the number of licenses is the restriction of the location and character of places where liquor may be sold. In the past, saloons were prohibited in some states within a specified distance of schools and churches. While location must be subject to control, we believe the restriction should be an administrative measure rather than a legislative enactment. This will enable the state licensing authority to grant or refuse licenses on a rational basis after consulting neighborhood and community desires, and after considering the requirements of local zoning laws. While the license law should also prohibit screens, upstairs rooms and back rooms, and the presence of gambling and slot machines, and should establish general regulations with regard to lavatories, et cetera, the licensing authority should be given wide power to expand and enforce such legal provisions through appropriate rules and regulations.[4]

Fifth: Licenses should be classified to recognize the inherent differences between beer, wine and spirits as problems of control.[5] One of the most satisfactory license classifications in this country before prohibition was in Massachusetts where seven kinds of licenses were provided.[6]

---

[3] Massachusetts (beer law) Laws 1933, Chapter 120, Section 6; Rhode Island, Laws of 1933, Chapter 2013, Section 16.

[4] The use of screens is prohibited in the new laws of the following states: Connecticut (taverns only) (Laws 1933, Chapter 140, Section 25), Missouri (beer law) (Laws 1933, Page 256, Section 13139Z8), Nebraska (beer law) (Laws 1933, Page 85, Section 10), New Jersey (beer law) (Laws 1933, Chapter 85, Section 3) and Rhode Island (Laws 1933, Chapter 2013, Section 27).

[5] See page 29.

[6] Massachusetts Revised Laws, 1902 – Ch. 100, Sec. 18.

Somewhat on the lines of this precedent a classification like the following might be desirable:

A. For Off-Premises Consumption—
    Class I   Beer to 3.2 per cent.[7]
    II   Natural wines up to 10 or 12 per cent.
    III   Spirits and all other alcoholic beverages.
    IV   Medicinal beverages and tonics, containing spirits.
    V   Undenatured, industrial alcohol.
B. For On-Premises Consumption—
    VI   Beer to 3.2 per cent.
    VII   Natural wines up to 10 or 12 per cent.
    VIII   Spirits and all other alcoholic beverages.
C. For Manufacture and Processing—[8]
    Divided as under A
D. For Commercial Transportation—
    Divided as under A, but distinguishing between shipments within the state and across state lines.

In many, if not most of the states, not all of these licenses will be either necessary or desirable, particularly classes VII and VIII. In any case the conditions attaching to each of these classes should, for

---

First Class—To sell liquor of any kind to be drunk on the premises.

Second Class—To sell malt liquors, cider and light wines containing not more than fifteen per cent of alcohol, to be drunk on the premises.

Third Class—To sell malt liquors and ciders, to be drunk on the premises.

Fourth Class—To sell liquors of any kind, not to be drunk on the premises.

Fifth Class—To sell malt liquors, cider and light wines containing not more than fifteen per cent of alcohol not to be drunk on the premises.

Sixth Class—Licenses to retail druggists and apothecaries to sell liquors of any kind for medicinal, mechanical or chemical purposes only, and to such persons only as may certify in writing for what use they want them.

Seventh Class—Licenses to dealers in paints or in chemicals to sell alcohol for mechanical, manufacturing or chemical purposes only.

[7] Though this chapter does not deal with light beer and wine, they are included in this classification in order to make it all-inclusive.

[8] The state regulations should be prepared in coöperation with the federal government and supplemented by federal regulations.

reasons stated in Chapter II, follow different principles. For example, in our judgment beer to 3.2 per cent (Classes I and VI) should be subject to little restriction. The heavier beers and wines should be purchasable by the package for home consumption (Class II), but for on-premises consumption by the glass, only with meals (Class VII). We think it undesirable to combine Classes VI and VIII. Most of the restrictions with regard to back rooms, screens, etc., apply only to Classes VII and VIII.

It is perhaps unnecessary to point out that any state admitting VIII is running the gravest kind of risk. It is through the open door of these two classes that the saloon will endeavor to find its way back into our social life. The sale of higher alcoholic beverages for on-premises consumption threatens the return of evils which in the past have defied control, and only the affirmative pressure of public opinion in a given state or community could possibly justify the admission of this type of license.

Sixth: The hours of sale of liquor, particularly for on-premises consumption (Classes VI, VII and VIII), should be carefully regulated. The English plan of stopping such sale and closing places of sale for two hours during the afternoon appeals to us as desirable. A closed period in the afternoon is of no inconvenience to normal consumption, but is extremely useful in preventing "soaking" and the excessive use of alcohol. The hours for Sundays, holidays, etc., will require still further restriction. It must be remembered, however, that a too stringent limitation of hours will play into the hands of the bootleggers. This is to be avoided, particularly in the immediate future, while the organized bootlegging system is being stamped out.

Seventh: Licenses issued for the retail sale of liquor should run not only to the person who sells, but to the *premises* where the liquor is sold. Revocation of a premises license is a far more effective weapon of control than is the revocation of an individual license.

Eighth: The license law should prohibit, as far as possible, all sales practices which encourage consumption. This would include treating on the house, sales on credit or IOU's, bargain days, and reduced prices previous to elections.

Rules are also necessary forbidding sale to minors, habitual alcoholics, paupers, mental defectives and to anyone who is drunk.[9]

Ninth: Advertising should, where possible, be rigidly restricted or forbidden. Six states have already passed such laws.[10]

The problem cannot be solved entirely by legislation, since subtle and inferential advertising may meet the letter but not the spirit of the law. The radio and nationally circulated publications are also beyond complete state control. None the less, each state should outline its liquor advertising code. These codes should be as nearly uniform as possible so that advertisers may readily conform. With this in mind, we suggest as a basis for discussion some such program as the following:

1. Newspaper and magazine advertising to contain nothing beyond the name, the address, the date of incorporation of a manufacturer or dealer, a coat of arms or trade-mark, and a description in the simplest terms of the article or articles dealt in, such as "Kentucky Rye Whiskey," or "Cointreau," or "Italian Vermouth."

2. All additional advertising matter, including slogans, to be prohibited except on approval of the state licensing board.

3. All outdoor advertising, except on the premises where sold or manufactured, to be prohibited. All outdoor electric or projecting signs to be further regulated by local fire, zoning and sign legislation.

    Content of advertising to be under the same restrictions as newspaper and magazine advertising.

4. All advertising matter attached to vehicles owned by manufacturers, distributors and dealers to be subject to the same

---

[9] These provisions are generally included in legislative proposals and in some instances, as in Connecticut (Laws 1933, Chapter 140, Sections 56 and 57) and Rhode Island (Laws 1933, Chapter 2013, Section 70), an order of interdiction is prescribed for persons receiving town aid and for those whose relatives have filed complaint. In Connecticut, not only is the sale of alcoholic beverages prohibited to minors (Section 59), but a penalty is also provided for inducing minors to procure liquor (Section 60).

[10] Delaware (Laws 1933, House Bill 312, Section 9), Iowa (beer law) (Laws 1933, Chapter 37, Section 34), and Ohio (beer law) (Laws 1933, Senate Bill 346, Section 4) provide that all advertising (all outdoor advertising in Iowa) shall be under the supervision of the liquor commissions, while Oklahoma (beer law) (Laws 1933, Chapter 153, Section 2) and Wyoming (beer law) (Laws 1933, Chapter 92, Section 6) provide that there shall be no advertising by any person dealing in alcoholic beverages.

restrictions as publication advertising.

5. All advertising through the use of calendars, pencils, golf balls, thermometers, free samples, cut-rate sales, etc., to be prohibited.

6. Radio advertising to be subject to the general rules outlined for publications.

The penalties to be provided by law should be moderate, particularly during the first few years while definite standards are being determined. No restrictions should be imposed upon the advertising of 3.2 per cent beer. The restrictions as a whole should apply not alone to the advertisers, but also to the advertising media, in order to reach the problem of indirect liquor advertising by ginger-ale companies, refrigerator companies and others who sell accessories.

We believe that such a code will be sufficiently elastic to meet the legitimate demand of the trade and at the same time to permit of enforcement. Undoubtedly, the most serious objections to these restrictions will come not from the liquor dealers themselves, but from the advertising agencies, the billboard and electric sign companies and even from some newspapers and magazines. These groups should realize, however, that unless reasonable restrictions are willingly accepted, there will undoubtedly be in the near future a complete prohibition of all kinds of liquor advertising, with extensive federal legislation as well as state codes.

Tenth: In addition to the foregoing possibilities, an effort may be made under the licensing system to control prices and profits. In Rhode Island, where legislation of this type has already been passed, the price control provision has been extended to the wholesale rather than to the retail trade.[11] Experience in this field is limited, but experiment may be fruitful. For example, the licensing authority could be authorized to establish minimum and maximum prices for the sale of liquor, to require uniform systems of accounts to be kept by liquor dealers, and to capture as an excise all profits in excess of a specified rate or a percentage of all profits.[12]

---

[11]Rhode Island Laws of 1933, Chapter 2013, Section 49.

[12]See Chapter VII.

Local Option

Under the license system as it operated before prohibition, the voters in individual cities and counties were often given the right to determine whether their communities should be "wet" or "dry." This is what is meant by local option. Though the British Royal Commission in 1931 condemned local option so far as its extension to England was concerned, we none the less believe that the case for such a policy in the United States, within proper limits, is too clear to need defense.[13] In recognizing the diversity of sentiment that exists within the state, in trying to adapt the law to the opinion of the community so as to gain its support, local option marked a wise and shrewdly conceived development. Past experience, American practice in other fields – indeed, our very system of local government – point to its essential usefulness. With the repeal of national prohibition, we believe there should be a reestablishment of this cardinal principle.

It is desirable, however, to make important changes in the practical workings of the principle to meet present-day conditions. Vast changes in American life have occurred since the idea was first developed. Chief among these is the wide use of automobiles. Moreover, local option showed various defects even before 1920. To meet old weaknesses as well as new conditions, it seems to us that special attention should be given to the following points:

1. *The area of local option.* Existing political divisions are manifestly unsatisfactory. In some cases they are too large, including urban and rural elements; while in other cases they are too small, dividing homogenous metropolitan areas. New local option areas, based on factual surveys, are manifestly a necessity.
2. *The subject matter of local option.* Although voters should not be asked to vote on problems that are too complicated or involved, the choice between "wet" or "dry" is too narrow.

---

[13]The Royal Commission said: "It is contended that questions relating to the sale of intoxicants are specially suited for local decisions by popular vote. We do not accept this contention." Cmd. 3988 Par. 438.

The automobile has upset the possibility of certain types of local restriction, and this condition should be frankly realized. In our judgment, the appropriate options should relate to:

(a)   The problem of on-premises consumption, i.e., licenses of Classes VI, VII and VIII.[14] Each class should be voted on separately, "yes" or "no."

(b)   The problem of local retail shops, i.e., licenses of Classes I, II and III. Each class should be voted on separately, "yes" or "no." We do not believe that local option should extend to the control of manufacturing or transportation, i.e., classes under C or D.[15]

3. *The stability of local option.* One of the most unfortunate features of local option under pre-prohibition conditions was the instability of community mood and decision. Frequent changing back and forth has the tendency to drive responsible persons out of the business. It forces the remaining proprietors into politics, and by increasing the financial hazards, provides an incentive to dealers to push sales inordinately. Partly to introduce greater stability, we have already suggested the creation of appropriate areas and the provision of a variety of options. We believe it desirable also to require that local option votes be at special elections, so that the question of liquor may not be involved in general politics. A matter thus determined should not be subject to reconsideration for three or four years.

Defects of the Licensing System

In the foregoing pages we have endeavored to present the most promising principles and devices appropriate to the license system of liquor control. While many of these suggestions may

---

[14]See page 31.
[15]See page 31.

seem chimerical, and difficult of enforcement, it must be remembered that the licensed dealers may perhaps be inclined to assist in enforcing the law against illegal practices and illicit trade competition. National prohibition has been a hard school. The example of government sales agencies successfully operating in the Canadian provinces, and possibly in the future in some of our states, will be a constant threat of what may happen if the old abuses return. It is not entirely inconceivable, therefore, that a chastened liquor trade, operating under a sound licensing system, may come to see that restraint and honest cooperation with license control is the policy dictated by a truly enlightened self-interest. However, over against this promising new factor must be set the irresponsible codes of lawlessness of the bootleggers, many of whom will now be licensed. It is difficult to estimate in advance the comparative influence of these conflicting forces.

A liquor licensing plan which might include all the desirable features outlined above must still be regarded as defective in four important and, we believe, vital respects. Its primary weakness consists in the preservation of the private profit motive, which would be threaded through the entire business from manufacture to ultimate local sale. Students of liquor systems and proponents of plans have differed widely in their analyses and in their recommendations, but there is general agreement that the elimination of the profit motive, if it can be accomplished, is, for America at least, the most promising road to successful control. A greedy liquor traffic looking only for larger profits will circumvent and evade any system of license defenses which ingenuity can erect. Even if through legislation, an arrangement could be contrived, as we have suggested above, by which prices are fixed and profits are limited, it would encounter the inescapable hazards of corruption and run the serious risk of bogging down in the minute details of regulation.

In the second place, any licensing system tends to project the whole question into politics and to keep it there. Indeed, it compels the traffic to be in politics for self-protection. The licensing body becomes a powerful political engine. Every licensee, as well as every manufacturer who sells to a licensee or has any interest in the business, begins to marshal his own political strength to serve his own ends. A multitude of private traders means a multitude of opportunities for political favoritism. Even if the initial results were fairly satisfactory under severely restrictive licensing arrangements, the test would come later as vendors learned the ropes. Then would appear the annual flood of bills in the legislature proposing amendments designed to relax the license system's stranglehold on licensees. The advocates of restriction would counter with their lobbies, and the whole miserable conflict would again be upon us.

In the third place, a system of licenses to private traders is, theoretically at least, incompatible with any idea of temperance education. While individual vendors of the better class may from motives of self-interest and conscience join with temperance forces in curbing individual abuse, this is as far as they will go. They will not welcome a general falling off in consumption. If we assume, first, that it is of prime importance to avoid stimulation of demand for alcoholic beverages and, second, that private traders will in fact endeavor to stimulate demand, then we are faced with a contradiction which plainly cannot be reconciled within a single system of control.

There is no reliable method of forecasting what will be the normal per capita consumption of alcoholic beverages with the repeal of the Eighteenth Amendment. But we are confident that the rate of consumption is a modifiable phenomenon, and that a sustained program of education would result in a substantial reduction of consumption below the level that would be reached if temperance education were ineffectively promoted. Whatever method of control is adopted, it is inescapably clear that its degree of success will depend in no small measure upon the kind of opposition raised against it. And this opposition will surely come in subtle as well as open form from those business interests which would suffer most from curtailment of trade. To promote temperance education and at the same time to tolerate a system of sale pulling in the opposite direction is scarcely an intelligent method of approach.

In the fourth place, to adopt the license method is to follow the easy path, but it is a path which affords no sure retreat if the system proves unsatisfactory. For the establishment of a licensed liquor trade means the deep intrenchment of a far-flung proprietary interest. This interest would have a large capital investment to be protected at all costs. Buildings, leases, fixtures, inventories, stocks and bonds—representing millions of dollars—would require defense against those who in the public interest might threaten curb or reduction. The question of property rights would at once be involved, and the states adopting the license system would be faced, as England is faced today, with a widespread disinclination seriously to disturb a business into which so much money had been put.

Moreover, such a vested interest is bound to employ aggressive tactics in its own defense. Liquor trade associations, open and disguised, would continuously oppose every restriction of opportunities to sell. Manufacturers, wholesalers and retailers, through their respective associations, would unite in resisting disestablishment of retail selling outlets whenever attempts were made to eliminate a portion of them either by local option votes or by reduction of the total number of licensed places.

In this respect the experience of England is illuminating. The Royal Commission on Licensing (England and Wales) in 1931 pointed out that when the Act aiming at reduction of liquor licenses was passed in 1904, it was estimated by supporters of the bill that possibly 48,000 of the 99,478 licenses in existence would be suppressed in 20 years. Although generous provisions were made for compensation of owners, the net decrease in twenty-six years was only 22,143.[16] The comment of the Royal Commission is pertinent: "The Trade has now developed an elaborate defensive organization. The broad basis of criticism against this organization is that its policy is dominated by one object—to sustain the sectional interest of the trade to the exclusion of all other interests, national or otherwise. This characteristic is specially condemned as antisocial in the case

---

[16]Report of the Royal Commission on Licensing (England and Wales) 1929-31, p. 25.
[17]Ibid. pp. 75-76. The Commission observes that "we have some sympathy for this general angle of view, even though we think that the position has to some extent been thrust upon the liquor trade."

of a trade whose wares are represented as potentially dangerous to public welfare."[17]

Under license system, the will to survive permeates every department of the trade, and the means to press a tenacious fight for survival are abundant. As proposals to dismember any part of the liquor selling business become more threatening, the entire trade combines more solidly to protect itself. In brief, a licensed liquor trade, once established, cannot easily be dislodged.

With the passing of the Eighteenth Amendment, the American states are free to make a fresh start. Only the public welfare needs to be considered. There are no property interests that have to be defended, no investments demanding protection, no organized retail trade associations to fight. For a state, confronted with this opportunity, deliberately to tie its own hands by establishing an intrenched business that will seek in its own protection to thwart every limitation and block every change, would seem to be the height of folly.

•   •   •   •   •

Perhaps by a herculean effort we could temporarily hold in check the instinct of business to increase its profits, but we would be gratuitously assuming a task that in the long run promises nothing but disappointment and defeat. Unless that motive is divorced from the retail sale of spirituous liquor, unless society as a whole can take over this business in the protection of its citizens, the future, at least in America, holds out only the prospect of an endless guerilla warfare between a nation fighting for temperance and a traffic that thrives on excess.

Chapter Five

THE AUTHORITY PLAN

Sᴛᴀᴛᴇ Mᴀɴᴀɢᴇᴍᴇɴᴛ ᴏꜰ ᴛʜᴇ ᴅɪsᴛʀɪʙᴜᴛɪᴏɴ ᴀɴᴅ sᴀʟᴇ ᴏꜰ ᴀʟʟ ᴛʜᴇ ʜᴇᴀᴠɪᴇʀ alcoholic beverages is the recognized alternative to the license system in states which decide to legalize the sale of liquor. There have been, and are in existence, various kinds of government management. The more widely known examples are the Quebec Liquor Commission and similar commissions in other Canadian provinces; the so called Bratt System of Sweden; the Norwegian and Finnish wine and alcohol sales monopolies; and the Carlisle State Management Scheme in England. To list these examples is to indicate the variety of terminology employed to describe government liquor monopolies. Though we have examined the more important plans in operation, we shall not endeavor in this report to describe and analyze them. This has already been done so many times that repetition here is unnecessary.[1] It is the purpose of this chapter to present a concrete plan for a state liquor monopoly applicable to American conditions, embodying ideas drawn from the best plans in operation; to compare this plan with the license system as a means of control; and to present our conclusions and recommendations.

Aɴ Aᴍᴇʀɪᴄᴀɴ LɪQᴜᴏʀ Aᴜᴛʜᴏʀɪᴛʏ Pʟᴀɴ

By a state liquor monopoly we mean, in its simplest terms, a system by which the state government takes over, as a public monopoly, the retail sale, through its own stores, of the heavier alcoholic beverages for off-premises consumption. Foreign experience

---

[1] See Appendices II and III.

and our own analysis of the problem here and abroad indicate that such a system makes it possible adequately to meet an unstimulated demand within the limits of conditions established solely in the interests of society. The state organization in charge of such a system might properly be called the "State Alcohol Control Authority." Hereafter in this chapter we shall speak of this organization as the Authority. In the following pages the tasks and appropriate powers of this new organization are outlined in some detail, so that the idea behind the plan may be completely understood.

Scope of the Authority's Task

The primary task of the Authority would be the establishment of a chain of its own retail stores for the sale of the heavier alcoholic beverages by package only. These stores should be so located as to meet normal demands without violating the desires of individual sections of the state to have no such stores in their localities. At the present time, we believe, it is neither desirable nor necessary for the state to assume similar management of the manufacturing side of the trade. Virtually all the individual and social evils of the liquor traffic arise from an inadequately regulated and overstimulated retail sale. The supplies that the Authority needs in its stores it can readily purchase direct from the manufacturers. From an administrative standpoint, also, manufacturing is complicated and requires capital and skill, while retail distribution is, in comparison, simple. It would be necessary, of course, for the Authority to place under regulation all manufacturing and all transportation (so far as it is legally permissible) and to require a complete record of production and shipments. The Authority would also be the official agency for gathering facts and making studies bearing on the liquor problem, on its own administration and on related matters.

In order that the functions to be performed by the Authority may be definite, it is necessary that they should be specifically enumerated in the laws and that appropriate rights and powers should be conferred.

Powers of the Authority

On the basis of experience elsewhere, the following powers would be necessary for the discharge of the Authority's responsibilities:

1. The exclusive right within a state to sell or control the sale of all alcoholic beverages which contain spirits; all wines known as fortified wines, the alcoholic content of which exceeds that produced by the natural fermentation process; and all fermented products, such as beers and ciders, containing more than 3.2 per cent of alcohol by weight.

2. The right to lease or own and to operate retail shops for the sale of those beverages by the package to the ultimate consumer for off-premises consumption, except that the Authority should be bound to abide by the decision of communities which vote to exclude the retail sale of any or all alcoholic beverages under local option provisions.

3. The right to lease or acquire by purchase or condemnation and to operate warehouses, blending and processing plants and other facilities as may be required.

4. The right to fix prices on its goods and to change prices at will.

5. The right to establish in its discretion a system of personal identification of purchasers.

6. The right to establish regulations and to issue permits to owners or occupants of establishments to sell beer and naturally fermented wine or cider in sealed bottles or containers for off-premises consumption.

7. The right to establish regulations and to issue permits to hotels, restaurants, clubs, railway dining cars, and passenger boats, for the sale of beer, with or without meals, and for the sale of naturally fermented wine or cider to be consumed with meals on the premises.[2]

---

[2] As a matter of economy and convenience, the law should enable the Authority to grant holders of these permits the right to purchase the permitted alcoholic beverages directly from the producers or from producers' agents, provided the Authority is empowered to require a complete reporting to it of all such direct purchases.

8. The right to require private business concerns to certify the quantities of alcohol and alcoholic beverages manufactured in the state, and the amounts shipped into, within, and from the state, regardless of the purposes for which used; this to be worked out in cooperation with the federal government.
9. The power to hold hearings on complaints about matters in dispute, including the power to subpoena witnesses and records and to make binding decisions.

That these are broad powers there is no denying. But powers as extensive have been conferred on similar bodies in jurisdictions where the democratic principle is as strongly entrenched as it is with us. In handling a problem as hazardous as the liquor trade, a broad grant of power, under ultimate legislative control, is the only effective method.

It is to be noted that no reference is made in this list of powers to the sale of heavier alcoholic beverages by the glass for on-premises consumption. Such sale is inevitably fraught with danger to the public interest. It is our hope that a generous provision for the on-premises sale of beer and natural wine, together with sale of stronger beverages by the package in the Authority's shops, would be accepted as adequate in most jurisdictions by a preponderant majority of people.

Organization of the Authority

The Board of Directors

The Authority should be administered by a Board of Directors of perhaps three members serving full time and engaging in no other occupation. The salaries of the Board members should be fixed at a sufficiently high level to insure acceptance of appointment by persons of outstanding ability. The term of office should be long enough to give the directors an opportunity to develop fully the policies they have begun. A long term promotes independence as well as freedom from concern about reappointment. We suggest, therefore, that Board members be appointed by the Governor for nine years with overlapping terms, subject to removal only for cause.

The Board would be concerned with the determination of all matters of policy entrusted to it by law, and with the settlement of complaints and disputes. In determining policy and in making the required rules and regulations, its duties would be quasi-legislative in nature. In hearing complaints with regard to the working of any phase of the plan or in trying charges against its employees, its duties would be of a quasi-judicial character. A Board of at least three members would be required in the exercise of these powers.

Managing Director

In connection with an undertaking of such magnitude as the proposed Authority is bound to be, a distinction should be made between the policy-determining function and the executive function. A chief executive officer, called perhaps a Managing Director, would seem to be necessary to carry on the work of the Board in accordance with the spirit and aims of established policies. The Managing Director's relation to the Board should be similar to that of a corporation chief executive to his board of directors. It would probably be wise to give him the right to appoint all subordinate officers with the approval of the Board.

Internal Organization

The operating organization would conceivably have the following principal units: (1) Division of retail shops and agencies, (2) division of permits, (3) treasury, (4) bureau of inspection, (5) central purchasing bureau, (6) bureau of personnel, (7) bureau of records and statistics. Provision should also be made for a small legal staff, a chemist and others. All employees required to man these units should be selected on a merit basis in accordance with a routine established by the Managing Director.

In outlining this organization we have intended to give only general suggestions. The Authority should be free under the law to create its own organization. The point we wish to stress is that the Authority Board members should refrain from attempting the detailed management of operations, entrusting this function to a competent, high-salaried, permanent and loyal executive. If such a Managing Director is chosen, the details of organization should be left to him.

Flexibility

We emphasize again that in the creation of the Authority and in the definition of its powers broad latitude must be provided. All things considered, we believe it to be preferable to place reliance upon the spirit of the enabling legislation rather than upon a multitude of legal prohibitions, limitations and directions, which would cripple and thwart the Authority at every turn.

Competent, socially-minded men of unblemished integrity, who, within the spirit of the law, set themselves to administer a liquor control system, would, if given wide power, doubtless make a first-class job of it. They would not need a mass of legal restrictions to tell them what they should not do. In fact, competent administrators could not work consistently toward a goal if they were hampered at every turn in the exercise of discretion. For these reasons we urge that the Authority be invested with ample powers, that the Board members be made secure in their tenure of office, and be left free to adjust their policies and regulatory procedures to social needs.

Relation of the Authority to the State Government

The State Alcohol Control Authority should be created as a special branch of the state government. It should, however, like a public corporation, be free from the traditional departmental restrictions which govern purchases, appropriations, personnel and similar business matters. The nature of its work, embracing as it does both regulatory and commercial functions, makes this essential. Within the definite tasks and responsibilities established by law, the power of the Authority would be plenary. Although as a matter of form the Authority should be designated as being within the executive department of the state government, the power of the Governor would extend only to the appointment of its members. The approval of its budget should rest with the Board of Directors, as in a private corporation. The same principle would apply also to all matters having to do with its finances, personnel and purchases. The only exception to this principle would be the right of the state auditor or comptroller to audit the transactions of the Authority at the direction of the Governor.

There is in this independence nothing novel or untried. In fact, it is fast being accepted as the logical method of organizing the management of a large-scale public enterprise which is (a) self-supporting through the ordinary commercial processes of buying and selling or charging for service, (b) which is operating in a new and experimental field, (c) which must be accorded a broad delegation of powers and (d) which must be guaranteed freedom from the routine of bureaucracy, the instability of current elections and the annoyance of spoils politics. It is these considerations that have led to such independent enterprises as the London Passenger Transport Authority, which owns and operates all the tram, bus, and underground transport facilities of London. The British Broadcasting Corporation is another such authority. In this country we have similar organizations in the Port of New York Authority, various bridge authorities and the recently organized Tennessee Valley Authority. The endeavor to control liquor through the handling of retail sales is, from the standpoint of management, a similar problem. It will be self-supporting; it requires experiment; it entails a broad delegation of powers; and it must be given a fair trial free from departmental, political or spoils interference. The appropriateness of the Authority device and of its peculiar detachment from the ordinary departmental scheme is well attested by the fact that within the last quarter of a century no nation or state, which has adopted this plan of liquor control, has abandoned it.

This does not mean, however, that the Board of Directors in most states would not rely heavily upon the help of existing state departments. Coöperation is essential. Such staff agencies as the state civil service, accounting, purchasing and budget offices should not be unnecessarily duplicated. But the decision should be left entirely to the discretion of the Authority. The Authority would undoubtedly establish only a small inspectional service of its own, because of the assistance to be derived from the state and municipal police, the state health inspectors and the tax department. Here again the power of the Authority should be complete to determine its course of action. There is no other way of fixing the responsibility.

The plan for financing the Authority, whether by appropriations, as is true of the Tennessee Valley Authority, or by state bonds, or by such other means as are permissible, would have to be determined in each state on the basis of its constitutional provisions. At quarterly intervals, following private corporate practice, the profits should be determined and paid over to the state treasury as dividends.

Disposition of Profits by the State

The profits of the Authority would, of course, be large. Wherever liquor sales monopolies have been established, or suggested, the proposal has appeared to "earmark" at least a portion of these profits for temperance education or other purposes. With this proposal we are in disagreement. We are convinced that no social activity of the government should be financed by specially designated taxes. Temperance education, charities, old-age pensions and any other welfare work should find their support in the general funds of the state in proportion to need and in competition with other demands. The profit policy of the Authority should be determined as a means of progressive liquor control, without regard to the revenue needs of hospitals, old-age pensions or temperance education. Earmarking of revenues is contrary to sound public finance. The profits of the Authority, therefore, should go directly into the state treasury without designation for any particular purpose.

SOUTH CAROLINA LIQUOR DISPENSARY PLAN

The South Carolina Liquor Dispensary Plan which was in operation from 1892 to 1906 is often referred to as though it were a state liquor monopoly essentially similar to the Canadian, the Norwegian, and the Swedish systems, or to such an Authority plan as we have outlined above. In spite of superficial similarities, nothing could be further from the facts. The South Carolina plan did not eliminate the profit motive from retail sales. The salaries of dispensing agents were made to vary with the amount of business done.[3] Moreover, these agents were in reality licensees, resembling private dealers under a license system. On approval of their applications, they received a "permit to keep and sell" alcoholic beverages supplied by the state board. This permit was limited to a single year.[4] The South Carolina plan made no effort to sever the central management from state politics. From 1892 to 1896 the state board of control was constituted of three elected state officials *ex officio*,[5] and from that time until 1904 the board and its executive officer were elected by the legislature.[6] As a result, from its inception, all appointments, especially of dispensers, were on a political spoils basis. "Party exigency was the father of the dispensary act."[7] Indeed the act was put forward in the first instance by the enemies of temperance and was adopted for the purpose of heading off state-wide prohibition. It was operated not as an instrument of social control but as an adjunct of "Pitchfork" Ben Tillman's political machine. Geared by law, as it was from the beginning, into current political controversies, and with its management placed in the hands of elected officials, no other result could have been expected. During the last five years of its operation, the control board frankly tolerated the existence of speakeasies, provided they purchased their supplies from the state.[8] In spite of this and many other defects in the plan, there is testimony of its temporary success in reducing drunkenness and crimes connected with the use of

---

[3] Committee of Fifty, *The Liquor Problem in Its Legislative Aspects*, by Wines and Koren, p. 168.
[4] South Carolina Laws of 1893, Act No. 313, Secs. 7, 8, and 9.
[5] The Governor, The Comptroller-General and the Attorney-General.
[6] South Carolina Laws, 1896, Act No. 61, Sec. 2.
[7] The Committee of Fifty, *op. cit.* p. 165.
[8] D. Leigh Colvin, *Prohibition in the United States*, p. 297.

liquor. But in the end it was a failure.[9]

In summary, the South Carolina Liquor Dispensary Plan was a state monopoly of the wholesale trade, grafted upon a scheme of local liquor licenses and of officially recognized, though illegal, speakeasies. The state board of control was welded by statute to the political system and the state bureaucracy, while the retail end of the trade was based directly upon private profit. It is thus evident that the South Carolina plan is in no way comparable to the state Authority plan which we have just outlined; and those who would dismiss the Authority idea because of its alleged failure in South Carolina would be well advised to study the fundamental divergencies.

THE STATE AUTHORITY VS. THE LICENSE SYSTEM IN OPERATION

The test of all plans is in their practical operation. It is not possible to compare American experience under a license system with experience under a state alcohol authority, because no American state has ever operated under the latter plan. Experience abroad, though suggestive, is, because of marked differences in social conditions, far from conclusive. Perhaps the most nearly comparable is the Canadian experience, under which in eight of the nine provinces both prohibition and license have been abandoned in favor of the state monopoly system. Our own careful investigations in Canada indicate that these systems are working with reasonable success. Although the Canadians have by no means solved all the difficulties, they are making distinct and intelligent progress. We found in Canada widespread approval of the underlying idea of state monopoly. Few desire to return to the license system.

Let us examine more specifically the inherent points of strength and weakness in the public monopoly and private li-

---

[9] Committee of Fifty, *op.cit.* pp. 147-180.

Colvin, *op.cit.* pp. 295-301.

Earl L. Douglas, *Prohibition and Common Sense*, p. 120.

Leonard Stott Blakey, *The Sale of Liquor in the South*, p. 19.

Annals of the American Academy of Political and Social Science, Nov. 1908, p. 545.

cense plans in dealing with such matters as sales stimulation, advertising, price control, character of liquor sales shops, temperance education and liability to graft and corruption.

It should be observed, first of all, that the objective is the same under both plans, namely, to place the sale of liquor under a series of restrictions devised to curtail excessive consumption. The only difference lies in the method of achieving this object. The licensing system endeavors to establish these controls through *negative* rules, regulations, conditions and taxes, *imposed from without*, upon *private* enterprise, which necessarily is conducted for *personal profit*. The State Authority plan endeavors to impose these controls through *positive management* from *within a public* enterprise conducted for the *benefit of society*.

Sales Stimulation

In what way do these differences in method of control affect the problem of sales stimulation? The answer is obvious. Under a state monopoly system the liquor would be sold directly by the state through a chain of stores and the profits turned into the state treasury, and that would be the end of it. No individual connected with the retail sale would gain one penny by reason of his sales, nor would his employment be imperiled if he failed to show good sales returns, as might be the case in private trade. In harmony with the underlying principle of the Authority, the salaried employees waiting on the customers in the various state stores would be under strict supervision not only to see that there was no encouragement of the sale of liquor, but to make sure that no beverages were sold in violation of the letter *and the spirit* of the regulations.

Under the license system, on the other hand, competing private dealers are under constant temptation to build up their sales and profits. The issuance of liquor licenses to private dealers presupposes the right to make a living by the sale of liquor. Since his livelihood is at stake, the private seller always has been, and always will be, interested in sales, and in nothing but sales.

Advertising

Advertising artificially stimulates the demand for alcoholic beverages. Though beer has been legalized only a short time and spirits are not yet legal, we are already overwhelmed with the skillful, persistent liquor advertisements of the modern sales psychologist. This is but a foretaste of what is ahead of us. All this is inconsistent with any idea of restricting the sale of liquor to an unstimulated demand. Although we have made a number of suggestions in the previous chapter, it is frankly difficult to see how in the long run such advertising can be definitely eliminated by state law under the license system. There are too many loopholes, too many indirect methods of advertising, too many national journals and broadcasting stations. Under the Authority plan, the opportunity for control of advertising is far greater. Indeed it could be practically eliminated if the public interest so demanded. In any event, the Authority could draft an advertising code and force its acceptance, either through refusal to buy from manufacturers who violated it or through a selective increase in the retail price of the products of an offender.

Price Control

The retail price level of alcoholic beverages not only determines profits, but also has a direct bearing on the amount of consumption and on the problem of the bootlegger. The prospective consumer desires a low price. The producer also wishes to set comparatively low prices to attract trade. The law enforcement officer is concerned lest extremely high prices of liquor encourage the bootlegger to undersell with its untaxed or adulterated products. The prohibitionist generally is one the side of high prices, for he believes that if liquor is expensive it will be placed out of the reach of many persons. The tax-levying authorities are not directly concerned with retail prices, but are eager to have large revenues.

Here is a knotty tangle of interests in the price of alcoholic beverages. Much, of course, will depend upon rates of taxation, and we are devoting a later chapter to this subject.[10] But inasmuch as the

---

[10]Chapter VII.

retail price of liquor is a central factor in regulating both legal and illegal consumption, the Authority can use its price-making power as one of its most effective instruments of control.

Rhode Island has enacted a law[11] giving to its licensing Board, called the Alcoholic Beverage Commission, power "to fix the wholesale prices of all such commodities [beverages] to be sold within this state or to be imported or brought into the state or exported therefrom, and to raise or lower such prices in whole or in part from time to time," etc. This legislation recognizes the crucial importance of regulating price; but one may doubt whether Rhode Island has proposed a workable method of accomplishing the result. It is not likely that a state liquor licensing board can exercise power to fix prices without running afoul of the strongest kind of opposition and interference from the private business interests involved. If prices are raised, those with stocks on hand will reap unearned profits; if they are lowered, losses will ensue. Under such conditions private dealers will not be inclined to stand idly by, nor will the public accept as reasonable a system which gives such fortuitous profits or losses to individuals. We anticipate, moreover, in connection with this type of legislation, a veritable field day of court actions. At the very least, between the licensing board and the private dealers a state of war will inevitably develop into which the legislature will be drawn.

In contrast, consider the Alcohol Control Authority's position. The Authority could fix prices without the slightest opposition from private business interests because the Authority would own the liquor. Through price control it could within limits modify sales volume at will. On the basis of results it could, if need be, change the prices again. It would even be possible for the Authority to sell certain products at a price below what would show a profit, if this step were thought expedient as a measure for promoting temperance through a change in drinking tastes. The Authority would be equally concerned with defeating the bootlegger and with avoiding the stimulation of consumption which might follow too low a level

---

[11]Rhode Island Laws of 1933, Chapter 2013.

of prices. The price of liquor is thus seen as a two-edged sword, but to avoid disaster the wielder of it must have exclusive possession of the hilt.

Character of Liquor Sales Shops

The surroundings in which liquor is sold have a great deal to do not only with the use and abuse of liquor, but with the community's attitude toward alcoholic beverages. The State Authority, having in mind a social rather than a profit objective, could set high standards in the physical character of its sales outlets. If the same thing were attempted under the license plan, it would have to be done by means of rules and regulations, or legal provisions which the state would endeavor to enforce through the police. The private dealer would, as in the past, seek to avoid, through subterfuge and influence, such invasions of his liberty.

What shall we say regarding the other regulations which might be imposed under a reformed licensing system, including such matters as the limitation of dealers to "responsible persons who have not been convicted of crime"; the limitation of the number of licensed places; limitations on business methods and limitations on the hours of sale? Under the Authority plan all these matters could be handled with far greater ease and probability of success. Consideration would be given to an effort to find efficient, reliable and loyal employees, not to question whether criminals were excluded from the trade. The pressure of applicants to enter the retail business would disappear. Stores would be established only when and where they were needed. Business methods would not be a problem of outside and distant control; they would be matters of inside management. In brief, with the elimination of the private profit motive most of the old difficulties would be removed.

Adaptation to Local Sentiment

While the liquor business of the future will be governed by state-wide policy, it should be adapted to meet the local sentiment of small sections and communities. This may in part be accomplished through "local option" in accordance with the suggestions already made in Chapter IV. These same suggestions apply to the operation of the Authority plan. But this adaptation to local preferences is, in our judgment, far from adequate to meet the present demands of the American people. What is needed now to supplement local option is a far more flexible plan under which reasonable liquor sale restriction will be worked out to meet local needs and desires, without resort to political campaigns and controversies.

A State Authority could, in fact, go further than the strict local option law by establishing, at the request of particular neighborhoods, dry zones within areas which voted as a whole to permit the sale of liquor. A city of 20,000 inhabitants, let us say, might vote to legalize liquor sales by only a small margin. Is liquor selling to be forced upon those areas of the city which are strongly opposed to it? Again, if the local option voting is on a countywide basis, a city might vote wet by a large margin and thereby prevail over the dry sentiment of surrounding rural territory. Divisions of this sort are bound to be common; and the majority vote, though determining the issue under the letter of a local option law, would, nevertheless, provoke much discontent in certain communities within the cities or counties involved.

The Authority could take these differences of opinion into account and in its own administrative discretion could meet the opposing views of lesser communities existing within the larger voting unit by declining to locate shops for the sale of liquor in those neighborhoods. Obviously, the Authority would, under no circumstance, place its shops on the border line of a dry area. This whole problem of border lines, so difficult to control under license, would disappear.

If community sentiment should turn against local sale of liquor after a period of trial, the Authority's shop could be closed merely by the signing of an executive order. There would be no wholesale or retail dealers to protest and demand compensation. Whatever loss might be involved would be absorbed in the Authority's total profit and loss account. Elimination of licensed private liquor-selling establishments, on the other hand, would result in serious financial loss to the individual seller and therefore, as in the past, would be the cause of frantic protest and political wire-pulling.

The Authority is conceived as an instrumentality for governing the sale of liquor in places where the majority of people demand the purchase of it, and not as an institution anxious to extend its sphere wherever business may be obtained. The whole emphasis of the Authority system is on limiting the sale to unstimulated demand and not on sales promotion.

Package Sale in Dry Areas

At this point mention should be made of the importance of permitting a State Authority to ship liquor by mail or express to persons living in dry areas, wherein retail shops are excluded by local option vote. This right of purchase is required primarily as a measure to suppress would-be bootleggers, but it has a secondary significance in that it would satisfy those who otherwise would be uncompromising opponents of the prohibition of liquor selling in their community. If the Authority were denied the right to fill orders in this way, a person living in dry territory would either go to a place where liquor is sold and there purchase what he required or he would have some other person make the journey for him. Naturally, the bootlegger would be the one most readily available to run the errand. Indeed, bootleggers are habitually foresighted and run their errands in advance. As a Norwegian official put it: "The bootlegger is always there even though the liquor shop is not."

Danger of Politics and Corruption

From an experience that is all too painful we are aware of the dangers of political influence and corruption under the license plan. Are these dangers not equally great under a State Management system? We think the answer can honestly be given in the negative. This opinion rests in part on experience elsewhere with state alcohol monopolies and in part on the revolutionary change which the elimination of private profit in retail sales brings into the entire situation. Politics and corruption entered the license system primarily because liquor dealers attempted to maintain and expand their sales. Licensed liquor dealers, driven on by the struggle for existence, endeavored to manipulate votes through every means, legitimate and otherwise. Corruption was almost inevitable. The license system turned loose a large number of individuals scattered over the state, particularly in the cities, each the center of a continuous endeavor, open and secret, to protect and extend his business. This was especially true in regions where the pressure to establish dry areas by local options was strong. Under a State Authority, the entire foundation is changed. Instead of a mobilized army of opposition to restriction of liquor selling, there is substituted a force of clerks, under chain-store accounting systems, who have nothing to gain from expanded sales.

Politicians will still be eager to control the patronage, and in some cases to determine the wet and dry areas, but they will not be able to lay their hands upon the profits. Under the Authority plan the entire responsibility for honesty and efficiency will be concentrated upon the Board of Directors and the Managing Director. There is, of course, no guarantee against dishonesty and abuse in any system; but the external regulation of recalcitrant private enterprise is clearly a more difficult task and more subject to graft than internal management by a responsible authority. This is doubly true of the liquor business.

CONCLUSION

On the basis of past experience in the United States and abroad, and the practical considerations we have just reviewed, we have come to the conclusion that the most satisfactory solution of the problem of alcohol requires elimination of the private profit motive in the retail sale of liquor. This cannot conceivably be accomplished under a license system, however rigid and well enforced. If we sincerely wish to meet only an unstimulated demand for alcohol, we can no longer leave to any individual a private stake in its retail sale. There is in the licensing of the private selling of liquor an irreconcilable and permanent conflict with social control.

The time is ripe for a change. Thirty years ago when the Committee of Fifty wrote its report,[12] it was far more difficult than it is today to conceive of the government participating in business. One objection to the South Carolina Dispensary Law, which came to its ill-fated end in 1906, was based on the fact that it was supposed to be "socialistic." Today this objection carries little weight. We have grown into a new age, and governments—national, state and municipal—have embarked on all types of business ventures to a degree that would have been impossible in the early years of the Twentieth Century. From the standpoint of the theory and practice of government there are plenty of precedents for this new type of liquor control. Governmental agencies own and operate bridges, tunnels, irrigation projects, power developments, shipping and a dozen other types of enterprise. To take such a step today in relation to liquor control is a far less difficult wrench than it would have been even a short generation ago.

Nor is the objection that the Authority Plan puts the government into the liquor business a valid one. It is based largely on emotion rather than on a realistic facing of facts. For better or for worse the liquor business is here. The private profit motive by which sales are artificially stimulated is the greatest single contributing cause of the evils of excess. It can be eliminated most effectively by state control. A compromise with any system of licensing is a halfway measure out of which at best only partial success can be brought. To insist on some arrangement that will minimize all the dangers of overindulgence, and at the same time to oppose the State Authority system because it identifies the government with the liquor business, is to be guilty of an inconsistency which cannot be justified on any logical or realistic grounds.

Moreover, the government always has been identified with the liquor business. For centuries it has regulated it in minute detail and has shared its profits through taxation. It has determined how and when liquor may be sold, the circumstances under which it may be sold, and the quality that may be sold. Such functions are inherent in

---

[12] *The Liquor Problem* – A Summary of Investigations Conducted by the Committee of Fifty, 1893-1903, p. 74.

every type of license regulation. To argue that the government can take no further step in the direction of control without giving the liquor business its endorsement and blessing is indefensible. The purpose of government is the promotion of social welfare, and the area of governmental activity in carrying out this purpose cannot be circumscribed by lines so artificially drawn.

We prefer the Authority plan because we believe that if given a fair and honest trial it stands a better chance of success than any other plan we have examined. This does not mean, however, that we regard it as an automatic cure-all for the evils associated with liquor. Nor do we offer it with a warranty that it is foolproof and will succeed under any conditions. It will not work under a régime of mismanagement and maladministration. Bad management and corruption are very real dangers. There will always be on hand certain representatives of the liquor interests, politicians and "fixers," eager to get control of the Authority in order to influence its policies and to further their own ends. There is no sure protection against such persons other than an alert public opinion focused upon a simple and responsible form of governmental organization. The proposed plan meets these requirements: It is simple in organization, it has direct lines of authority, and it is flexible enough to insure the making of changes, within the discretion of the directors, as experience points the need.

Now is the time to act if the State Alcohol Authority plan is ever to be tried in the United States. For this there are two convincing reasons: first, there is at present no legal private trade to be dispossessed; second, in the coming conflict with the bootleggers unity of command along the entire front—economic as well as legal—is half the battle won.

In summary, the principal merits which we conceive to be inherent in the State Alcohol Control Authority plan are these: It would effectively stifle the profit motive for enlarging liquor sales beyond a minimum demand. It would facilitate the control of advertising. It would provide freedom of action in regulating prices and conditions of sale, both as a means of checkmating the illicit dealer and as a method of curtailing the use of spirits. It would eliminate the saloon. It would minimize opportunities for the encroachment of political interference. It would keep clear the road for temperance education.

If this plan is adopted and honestly and competently administered, it should give a maximum degree of protection against the revival of age-old abuses known to licensed regulation, and against the more recent evils of a traffic unregulated by government and managed by law violators.

Chapter Six

THE AUTHORITY PLAN WITH ADAPTATIONS

MANY VARIATIONS EXIST IN STATE GOVERNMENTAL TRADITIONS IN THIS country, almost as many variations as there are states. There are different attitudes toward government ownership, different experiences in dealing with the liquor trade in the past, different problems relating to liquor control to be solved today and different levels of competence in governmental administration. All these factors will have a bearing upon the consideration of the Alcohol Authority plan which we have proposed. In this chapter we discuss three important modifications of the Authority plan which may conceivably make it more adaptable to different local needs and sentiments. These possible modifications are: *first*—the elimination of direct retail sales by the Authority through the creation of a private liquor sales corporation under the jurisdiction of the Authority; *second*—a plan for the establishment of agencies for the sale of spirits for on-premises consumption; *third*—a plan for the establishment of personal purchase permits.

I—THE SALES CORPORATION

Functions

In states where sentiment is in favor of a State Alcohol Authority but against direct government ownership and sale of alcoholic beverages, the sales function of the Authority could be lifted out of the scheme and transferred to a semi-private sales corporation. This sales corporation would be given monopoly rights within the state for the sale of spirits, fortified wines and heavy beers by the package for off-premises consumption. The corporation would buy beverages at home and abroad; it would blend, rectify and store. It would be called upon to deal with questions of financing purchases, credit and foreign exchange; to determine quantities of purchase, especially of wine in good vintage years, and varieties of brands to be handled; to decide whether to buy well-aged liquors which are ready for immediate consumption or unripened liquors at lower cost for storage over a period of years. There would be questions relating to the lease, purchase or construction of warehouses and retail shops. But the Alcohol Control Authority itself should govern the location of retail shops and all retail prices. But matters involving the exercise of business judgment and technique would thus be left to the management of business men in this incorporated subdivision of the Authority.

Organization and Finance

The sales corporation would be set up under a special corporate charter. There would be a small board of directors, consisting in part of persons elected by the stockholders, receiveing a small fee for each meeting, and in part of the members of the Alcohol Control Authority, *ex officio*. There would thus be directors representing private interests and directors representing the public interest. Predominant voting strength should be placed with the Authority representatives.

Provision should be made for a managing director, at a salary to be fixed by the board of directors. This officer would determine the appropriate administrative machinery and would appoint the subordinate personnel, as in a private business.

Cumulative limited-dividend stock, paying not in excess of 5 per cent under present conditions, should be authorized to finance the operations of the corporation. The original sale and subsequent transfers of stock should be restricted so as to prevent any of the stock and any of the directorships from falling into the hands of persons or corporations having a direct or beneficial interest in the liquor business. This is fundamental.

All profits beyond the cumulative dividend to stockholders,

which would undoubtedly be earned in the first few months of each
year, should accrue to the Alcohol Control Authority on a definite
quarterly basis from which they would pass to the state treasury.
The Authority should have the right to make periodic audits and
investigations of the operations of the sales corporation as a supplement to the regular outside audit, the publication of which should be
required by the by-laws.[1]

Pros and Cons

A sales corporation of this general character would serve a useful purpose in a state where public sentiment requires such a modification of the Authority plan. It could bring to the sales business
independent business sagacity, additional continuity and freedom
from political interference; and this solution might be satisfactory
to those who wish rigid control but do not want the government to
"enter the liquor business." While we regard this attitude toward
the relation of the government to the business as unjustifiable, we
recognize its force in some jurisdictions.

There are disadvantages and some dangers in this modification.
It makes the program more complex, although this circumstance
need not be over-emphasized since the only additions to personnel
are the directors of the incorporated subsidiary. The same sales organization with a director at the head would exist under either plan.
There is also a certain division of responsibility, and an acceptance
of the idea of checks and balances which has not been successful as
a rule in the regulation of utilities. Perhaps, however, the analogy
should be drawn in this case with holding companies, where inter-
locking directorates have been more successful. Finally, there is at
least the possibility of an anti-social attitude in relation to liquor on
the part of the private members of the board of directors. The definite limitation of the private profit motive, however, and the restrictions on stock ownership should help to safeguard the quality and

---

[1] This suggested system of a sales corporation is somewhat similar to the system obtaining in Norway
where the Vinmonopolet, a privately financed corporation, is managed by five directors appointed by
the Crown. The Vinmonopolet has entire charge of the distribution of spirits through its own stores (for
package sale) and through agents for on-premises consumption.

integrity of the directors.

II—Agencies for On-Premises Consumption

Public opinion in some states will undoubtedly demand the sale of all kinds of alcoholic beverages by the glass in hotels and restaurants. This will be true especially in large cities where a proportionately greater number of residents take their meals outside their homes. Similarly, the large transient population in our cities creates a special demand for spirituous drinks by the glass. Many hotel guests, if denied a cocktail with their meals, will buy a whole bottle of spirits for consumption in their rooms. We cannot blind our eyes to the popularity of cocktails in America. The growth of the cocktail habit has accompanied prohibition, and has indeed been stimulated by it, because bootleggers could more readily furnish alcohol in concentrated form suitable for making cocktails than they could the bulkier alcoholic beverages.

Established customs cannot be brushed aside at a stroke, and, in some places at least, it may be found necessary to provide for a closely regulated sale of spirituous beverages by the glass for consumption with meals. We return to our two fold aim in liquor control, which is to leave no legitimate need for the bootlegger to satisfy and, at the same time, to avoid stimulating the demand for liquor. If, for example, there is present an *insistent* demand for cocktails and liqueurs in a given locality, we may be sure that the bootlegger and the speakeasy will survive to satisfy it. The plain truth is that the legitimate need must be measured in terms of insistence of demand; it cannot be measured by what we might *hope* would be satisfactory. Thus measured, the legitimate need will be found to vary considerably from state to state and from locality to locality within a single state.

In what manner, then, could an Alcohol Control Authority regulate the sale of spirituous beverages by hotels and restaurants without bringing back the old saloon in a new disguise? We use the term "saloon" loosely, meaning the pre-prohibition barroom and its prohibition equivalent, the speakeasy. In states which feel the need of some liberalization of the plan as we outlined it in the preceding chapter, provision could be made for the Alcohol Control Authority to designate a rigidly limited number of restaurants and hotels as its agents in selling by the glass beverages of higher alcoholic content. These designations should be cancellable by the Authority at will. The spirits, fortified wines and beers heavier than 3.2 per cent would, of course, be procured by these restaurants and hotels only from the Authority stores.

Under this arrangement, whereby business establishments engaged in serving meals could occupy an agency relationship to the Authority or to the sales corporation, every opportunity would be preserved for holding in firm check the sale of the stronger alcoholic beverages by the glass. The Authority could impose upon its agents any regulations it might choose. The hotel or restaurant management would have no privately safeguarded rights in selling hard liquors; their only rights would be those delegated by the Authority and revocable at will.

Thus the Authority could fix prices and vary them as it chose; it could require any kind of accounting and reporting as to quantities of drinks sold, and food sold with them. It could fix rules governing the number of drinks permitted to be served to a customer at a single meal; it could regulate the hours at which the alcoholic beverages could be sold, and these hours might quite generally be less than the hours for the serving of meals; it could govern advertising; it could even set monthly quotas of the quantities of beverages to be purchased from the sales corporation at a wholesale price, and charge the full retail price for all quantities purchased in excess of such quotas. All these restrictions and more could be put into effect and altered by the exercise of administrative discretion. The Authority would decide and the agency would obey; or there would be no agency.

We are aware that the agency scheme would expose the Authority plan to great peril. The selection of a limited number of agencies from among many applicants would give rise to charges of favoritism, and attempted corruption would be a constant threat. If regulation were too liberally drawn, the abuser of alcohol would take advantage of his privilege of purchase; if too strictly drawn, the agencies would plead with political allies to curb the reputedly dictatorial Authority. The agency plan would be the rock upon which an Authority would be most likely to break. Particulary in metropolitan centers like New York and Chicago, the difficulties and temptations would undoubtedly be great. Notwithstanding these difficulties, however, it would not be impossible for an Authority that was strongly supported by public opinion to hold its ground in a rigorous supervision of its agencies. We cannot estimate the weight of the three interrelated factors of local demand for on-premises consumption, strength of the Authority's position and its degree of stability in public opinion. A delicate adjustment of these factors would be required, and each state would have to decide whether or not it could be made.

We hold no brief for this type of modification. It involves incalculable difficulties and dangers. We recognize, however, that, if public demand is thwarted by restrictions too narrowly drawn, the resulting abuses are apt to be more demoralizing than those which the law seeks to check.

III—The Purchase Permit System

We have discussed a possible liberalization of the sales monopoly plan in jurisdictions where liberality is unmistakably demanded. We now consider a modification which would have the opposite effect of imposing greater restriction on the purchase of spirits. A state may require that its alcohol monopoly sell only to persons who obtain a permit to purchase alcoholic beverages. This plan is followed in Sweden and in five of the Canadian provinces;[2] in Quebec, Norway and Finland, where state-controlled liquor monopolies were established subsequent to the repeal of prohibition, individual purchase permits are not required.

---

[2] Alberta, British Columbia, Ontario, Manitoba and Nova Scotia have the purchase permit plan.

Where the permit scheme is in force it applies only to liquors sold by the package at monopoly stores for off-premises consumption. Usually a limit is placed on the quantity of liquor a permit holder may buy at any one time, and sometimes a maximum amount is fixed which may be purchased within a month. The quantities of purchase are recorded on the permit card and are totaled by the month and year. Provision is made for the cancellation of a permit or for the reduction of the permitted purchase quota upon discovery that an individual holder has been an abuser of liquor. The principal evidences of abuse are drunkenness, commission of a crime while under the influence of alcohol, driving an automobile while intoxicated, bootlegging of purchases and neglect to provide for the family. This illustrative list of disqualifications could be extended if the varying practices in each country were included.

A great deal of controversy inevitably accompanies the operation of a liquor purchase permit scheme. Many persons are irked by it, but many others accept it willingly and defend it in the belief that it is a generally useful means of controlling abuses. Curiously enough, the permit system is opposed by a large number of anti-alcoholists in Sweden on the ground that possession of a permit is regarded by many holders as a badge of distinction, and that it places a premium on the right to buy liquor and thus tends to encourage the purchase of the total allowable quota.

Wherever the permit system is in operation certain evasions and misuses are found. Thus permits are transferred, for a consideration, to persons who are unable to obtain them; holders of permits purchase liquor for others; and bootleggers have a ready market in supplying persons whose permits are canceled. Application of the permit system's restrictive features in the case of persons who suffer, or cause others to suffer, from their excessive drinking involves the necessity for social welfare work, and alcohol control administrations are not likely to be well equipped for this kind of activity.

Experiment alone will reveal the value of such a permit system in our states. It might not work at all in populous areas where the bootlegging problem has been acute in recent years. On the other hand, a study of the operation of the system in the Canadian provinces of Ontario, Manitoba, British Columbia, Alberta, and Nova Scotia has shown that the police, magistrates, employers and social workers are strongly in favor of it and that they consider it to be an effective device for controlling those who are disposed to abuse their privileges under the liquor acts. The Canadian officials point out also that this system is valuable as a means of detecting those who purchase quantities in excess of their personal needs for the purpose either of bootlegging it by the drink or of selling it by package at hours when the government stores are closed.

Summary

One of the advantages of the State Authority plan is that it lends itself to adaptation to meet the peculiar conditions of individual states as well as the regional differences within each state. The quasi-private liquor sales corporation may be regarded as lessening the degree of participation of the government in the merchandising of liquor. Under some conditions, also, it may lessen the danger of political interference in this phase of liquor control. The local retail agency plan may be adapted to conditions in some states in order to meet the requirement for greater liberality in the sale of the stronger alcoholic beverages. The purchase permit system, on the other hand, imposes additional restrictions of a personal character. This scheme may be found desirable perhaps in some of the less populous sections of the United States.

We are not suggesting that these modifications of the Authority plan are desirable. All that we are saying is that they are possible. They can be used to meet public points of view that differ in different states. The Authority plan is elastic and is adaptable to divergent conditions.

Chapter Seven

TAXATION

Historically, taxes have been imposed upon alcoholic beverages both to provide revenue for the government and to reduce consumption. While these two objectives may be contradictory if carried to extremes, in most countries they exist side by side. A third objective, especially in the days before prohibition in the United States, was primarily punitive. It was felt by some that those who manufactured, sold or used alcoholic beverages were conniving with evil and that they should be punished with high special taxes.

Revenue as an Object

In designing new taxes for the reestablished alcohol beverage trade, should revenue be the primary objective? Campaign speeches and statements by budget authorities have frequently seemed to answer this question in the affirmative. With this answer we are in sharp disagreement. The fundamental objective should be not revenue but rational and effective social control. While this is not inconsistent with extensive revenues, we believe that liquor taxes should be levied, first of all, because the taxes will help to make the liquor controls more successful, and not because the Treasury needs funds. The fundamental motives should be broadly social, not narrowly fiscal.

Punishment as an Object

The repeal of prohibition marks also the end of punishment as a tax aim. If the moderate use of alcohol by those who desire it is generally accepted as legal, and as a matter of individual conscience, then such consumption cannot consistently be punished by high taxes. The justification for taxes must be based on other grounds.

Limitation of Consumption as an Object

In England, Denmark and other countries high liquor taxes have been successful in reducing the consumption of alcoholic beverages. They increase the price of spirits to a point at which many people cannot afford to buy. That is, of their own free will people decide to spend their money for something other than liquor, because such expenditure brings greater satisfactions. While this voluntary self-control, induced by high prices, is an indispensable and desirable measure, it has two distinct limitations: In the first place, it should not be applied to beer and light wines, since the consumption of light alcoholic beverages is least harmful and beer in particular is used by the lower income groups who cannot in justice be called upon to pay heavy taxes. In the second place, high taxes should be cautiously applied to spirits; such a policy increases the margin of profit for illicit manufacture and stimulates the sale of spirits by the moonshiners and bootleggers who have become so well established and organized under prohibition. In this matter the United States for the next few years will be faced with a unique situation. Our first task would seem to be to rid ourselves of organized bootlegging. A tax policy which defeats that immediate objective cannot wisely be maintained.

Effect of High and Low Taxes

It is illuminating to employ extreme figures to illustrate the effects of high and low taxation on the sale of alcoholic beverages. Let us suppose that American standard proof whiskey can be produced and sold, without excise, manufacturer's or retailer's taxes or licenses of any kind, for 45 cents per quart. Now suppose that this whiskey is taxed at not more than 5 cents per quart by federal, state and local governments combined. The retailer's price would then be 50 cents plus such profit as he could make, a total price, let us say, of $1.00. Assuming opportunities for purchase to be virtually unrestricted, we might expect the following results from such a prevailing price level:

1. The volume of consumption of spirits would be high because whiskey would be inexpensive and within the reach of nearly everyone.
2. The illicit manufacturer and the bootlegger would lose their market.
3. The system of liquor corruption of police officials, politicians and lower courts would disappear for lack of funds.
4. There would be little tax evasion, but the revenue would be small.

In contrast, let us suppose the tax to be $5.55 per quart, and the cost at retail, including profit, $7.00. We might then expect these results:

1. The consumption of legally produced whiskey would be small.
2. The moonshiner and bootlegger and the whole system of liquor corruption would flourish.
3. Substitutes more harmful than seasoned spirits would be increasingly used.
4. The revenue would be large in spite of the extensive illicit and untaxed liquor trade and the restriction of consumption.

It is clearly seen that high taxes cannot be employed in the United States at the present time as a means of alcohol control for the reason that they would furnish indispensable support for the illicit liquor business. Nothing will so quickly demobilize the moonshiner and the bootlegger, and throw into chaos the corrupt system they have created, as reasonable liquor taxes and low liquor prices. For the next three to five years, until the bootlegging régime which has developed under prohibition has been driven out of business, low taxes are imperative. It is with this in mind that other means of discouraging and controlling excessive consumption are recommended elsewhere in this report.

The Emerging Tax Chaos

Upon the repeal of the Eighteenth Amendment, federal, state and many local governments will doubtless proceed to impose all kinds of manufacturers' and retail taxes and licenses upon the liquor business. The rush to pass new tax laws is already underway. As in the past, this will produce an inconsistent mass of conflicting and overlapping tax legislation. The danger of the emerging tax chaos is, first, that considerations of fairness will be neglected; second, that the total tax levies will be so great as to continue the illicit liquor business; third, that wasteful duplication and conflicting policies in administration may render inefficient and ineffective the whole tax structure.

Under our federal form of government no easy solution of this problem is available. It would immensely simplify the entire matter of enforcement if the federal and state alcohol tax systems could be developed together as a unit, so that the rates of taxation would be uniform throughout the country; so that import duties might be properly related to domestic manufacturers' taxes; so that the total proceeds might be equitably distributed between the various governmental units; so that the total tax might not be so heavy as to place a premium on evasion, especially during the next few years; and finally, so that the administrative machinery might be simplified. But such a desirable solution can be brought about only through *prompt coöperative action between the states and the federal government.*

General Considerations

Though specific formulation of a coöperative scheme for the taxation of alcoholic beverages must be left to the taxing and other authorities of the governments involved, we may at least indicate in this chapter those principles which we believe should be the basis of the new liquor tax program.

Normal Business Taxes

Before proceeding to the discussion of the special taxes levied upon the manufacture and distribution of alcoholic beverages, it is well to remember that liquor manufacturers and dealers pay, in addition to these special taxes, the normal taxes imposed upon all businesses and individuals by the federal, state and local governments. These include the federal corporate income tax, the federal individual income tax, additional income taxes in certain states, wholesale and retail sales taxes in a few cases, automobile and gasoline taxes and, finally, state and local taxes on personal property and on real estate. These normal taxes which the liquor trade, like any other business, must carry, are no less onerous for liquor manufacturers and dealers than are the same taxes when falling on others. Though these normal taxes will not be discussed further in this study, it should be borne in mind that they are none the less a part of the entire picture.

Existing Special Liquor Taxes

There are two chief points at which special taxes on alcoholic beverages may be levied: first, manufacture; second, sale.

Manufacture is taxed by the federal government and by some of the states. The federal government bases its tax on two factors: a small flat license fee and an excise levy on the quantity produced. For example, the present levy on beer is a license of $1,000 and an excise tax of $5.00 per barrel. The excise tax on industrial alcohol is $1.10 per gallon. The excise levy is the significant and productive tax. Before prohibition, the state levies on liquor manufacture were confined to relatively light flat licenses. States are now, however, adopting excise taxes based on volume of production, following the plan of the federal government.

The *retail sale* of alcoholic beverages has been taxed primarily under state laws. Retailers pay a state or local license tax for the privilege of conducting the business. This may be levied against the dealer as a person, against the place of business as such, or against both. While the retail license taxes in the United States have almost without exception been flat taxes, bearing no relation to the amount

of business done, an effort has been made in some states to adjust
this inequality by relating the fee to the size of the city in which the
vendor had his place of business or to his gross receipts.[1] In some
jurisdictions abroad licenses have been auctioned off to the highest bidder or related to the rental value of the premises occupied—
methods which we do not commend.

The Incidence of Beverage Taxes

Who pays the liquor taxes? This question of incidence is often
overlooked in the discussion of the taxation of alcoholic beverages.
The classical tax economists, after much theoretical and practical
research and debate, are agreed that a manufacturers' tax, levied
equally upon all producers by volume, becomes a manufacturing
cost, and will, therefore, be passed on to the consumer along with
the other manufacturing costs.[2] While there are times of economic
instability when the manufacturer cannot pass on all his manufacturing costs or taxes, and thus operates at a loss, under normal conditions the manufacturer does not really pay the volume taxes at all.
He is merely the tax-collecting agent for the government.

Retail taxes when levied by volume or as sales taxes have the
same effect. They are a direct business cost and under normal conditions are passed on to the consumer.

A flat license tax, such as the $1,500 formerly paid annually in
New York City for a saloon license, is in quite a different category.
It may, or may only in part, be passed on to the consumer in higher
beverage prices. Where the number of licenses is sharply restricted,
so that there is no effective competition in prices, the liquor seller
has limited monopoly rights and can charge what the traffic will
bear. Under present conditions he would undoubtedly set his retail
prices to include the license tax, thus passing it on to the consumer.
Where, however, competition is keen, as a result of the existence of

---

[1] Laws of New York, 1917, Chapter 623; 1933, Chapter 180, Section 80. Illinois laws, 1933, p. 518,
Section 5. Nebraska Laws, 1933, p. 85, Section 8. Michigan, Public Act No. 64 (1933), Section 6.
[2] Seligman, E.R.A. *The Shifting and Incidence of Taxation*. Dalton, Hugh. *Principles of Public Finance*. Great Britain. Committee on National Debt and Taxation. Report. (Section IV, "The Incidence
and Effects of Existing Taxes.") Hobson, J.A. *Taxation in the New State*.

many distributors, the tax is not so easily passed on to the consumer.

In recent decades, both in this country and abroad, a new kind of taxation has been developed which cannot under normal circumstances be passed on to the consumer. This is the income tax; that is, a tax varying in accordance with the profits realized. Contrary to popular opinion, a tax on profits cannot generally be passed on to the consumer. While it is not possible in this study to demonstrate this point at length, it is to be accepted as axiomatic that, under normal competitive conditions of manufacture and sale, taxes by volume and by sales will, in general, be passed on to the consumer, while taxes on profits will be paid by the manufacturer or retailer and cannot be passed on.[3]

Many people have wondered how it was possible in the days before prohibition for so many distillers and brewers and saloonkeepers to become wealthy in spite of the large liquor taxes which they paid. A part of the answer is to be found in the fact that they did not pay the taxes levied against them. Because of the nature of the taxes it was possible to hide them in the prices and to pass them on to the consumer. This was inevitable, since we used a type of tax, and created through other restrictions a kind of semi-monopoly which made it easy and natural to shift the entire tax burden.

Tax Justice

In connection with liquor taxes, the problem of justice is not to be passed over lightly. The total burden of all federal and local special taxes on alcoholic beverages was, before prohibition, $500,000,000 a year. That is, it exceeded the total federal individual income tax of 1932 by 40 per cent. Under the taxes which we suggest below the total levy will be, we believe, approximately $700,000,000. This estimate, it must be remembered, does not include the normal federal, state and local taxes which the liquor trade will also bear. The method of distribution of so large a special tax burden is obviously a matter of grave social importance.

At this point, again, tax authorities and economists are agreed

---

[3] See references, page 74.

that all consumers' taxes on articles broadly used fall more heavily upon the poor than upon the rich. This is true of a tax on salt, for example, because a poor man's family will use as much salt as will the family of a wealthy person. The tax will, conceivably, form a considerable percentage of what the poor man has left for savings, while it will be only a very small percentage of what the rich man has left. The same principle is true of commodities like beer and wine. It does not apply with equal force to fancy beverages like champagnes, which presumably are consumed only by the wealthy. In contrast to income taxes, which are *pro*gressive, consumption taxes are *re*gressive, since they absorb and increasingly smaller percentage of total income as we go up the income scale.

In the days before prohibition, taxes on alcoholic beverages were heavy; they were so levied as to be passed on almost entirely to the consumer; and consumer taxes fall regressively, that is, more heavily at the bottom and less heavily at the top of the income scale. The question now arises: Do we wish to continue this system in the future? The tax legislation already enacted is of the same variety, though the addition of sales taxes and state manufacturers' taxes by volume indicates an even greater accentuation of regressive consumer taxes in the future. We frankly believe that this is a wrong road. We are convinced that a considerable part of the total taxes to be levied on the manufacture and sale of alcoholic beverages should be fastened upon the manufacturer and upon the retailer in such form that it cannot be shifted readily to the consumer. As has already been indicated, this can be accomplished by the use of profits taxation.

Reasonable Rate Structure

The tax rates on alcoholic beverages should obviously bear a reasonable relation to each other. This has not always been true in the past. An inter-relationship of this sort may be built upon a number of different bases. The more important are:

1. Variations in the content of alcohol. For example, standard whiskey contains twelve and a half times as much alcohol as

the present legal beer. On the basis of alcoholic content, the tax would vary as 12.5 to 1.

2. Variations in value. Standard whiskey of ordinary grade costs from 40 to 60 cents per gallon to manufacture, as compared with beer at 17 to 20 cents. The ratio is about 3 to 1.

3. Variations in the social desirability of consumption. This cannot be expressed in terms of exact fractions. From our point of view, however, there is no reason for an artificial restriction on light beers and light wines through the medium of price control. This, is however, desirable for the heavier alcoholic beverages. For spirits we think a handicap of 3 times the cost of manufacture is the safest point at which to begin. This will undoubtedly have to be modified later, as experience indicates.

4. Variations based upon ordinary versus luxury consumption; that is, upon the capacity to pay. Sparkling wines, champagnes, fortified wines and liqueurs are, in general, consumed by persons better able to pay taxes. They are not ordinarily consumed by the lower income groups. We have set a purely arbitrary ratio of 1, 5 and 8 as between spirits, liqueurs and champagnes, respectively.

The practical implications of these suggestions are shown in the table on page 81.

Recommend Tax Program

On the basis of the foregoing considerations, the following liquor tax program is recommended. With much hesitation we are presenting the general outlines of a system, together with specific tax rates, because there is no other method of conveying what we mean when we say, for example, that the tax on beer should be "low" or that the tax on spirits should not leave the bootlegger too large a profit margin. The suggested rates are illustrative only. They are offered as a basis for discussion and as a means of clarification.

Our suggestions are presented under two heads, which deal, first, with manufacture and, second, with retail sale.

Manufacturing Taxes

We recommend that the manufacture of alcoholic beverages be taxed exclusively by the federal government.

Under a system of free interstate commerce, uniformity in the taxation of manufacturers throughout the nation is desirable to maintain free competition. This uniformity cannot develop under independent state systems. Another important factor is the correlation of taxes on domestic manufacturers with duties on foreign import. The federal government alone has the power over import duties and should, therefore, be given control over the manufacturers' taxes as well, in order that a consistent and coherent plan may be developed. This is of special importance in dealing effectively with the smuggler. But the greatest difficulty arising from state taxation of the liquor manufacturers lies in the effects of differential tax rates. If New York, for example, placed a tax of $2.00 a quart on the manufacture of whiskey, while New Jersey levied a tax of but 50 cents, New York would drive its own distilleries to New Jersey and would create a thriving bootleg trade across the border. Unless we are to complicate our enforcement problems and immeasurably hinder the efforts of the states to bring the trade under control, the taxation of the manufacture of liquor must in the end be dealt with under a single federal policy.

A practical method of accomplishing this result is through an interstate and federal arrangement under which the participating states will agree to refrain from such levies while the federal government agrees to meet the costs of administration and distribute to the states, for example, 20 per cent of the amounts collected. Such distribution should, perhaps, be in proportion to the taxes collected within the several states.[4]

---

[4] As a matter of law, this can be worked out either through the joint designation of personnel to administer two identical taxes or through a compact plan and contingent federal aid appropriations. The joint designation of personnel, interstate compacts and conditional appropriations are all well-established devices. *State Government*, May, 1933. "A Selected Bibliography on Coordination of State and Fed-

Tax Rates on Manufacture

With regard to the tax rates on the manufacture of alcoholic beverages, we recommend:

1. That the excise tax on 3.2 per cent beer be placed at not more than $3.00 per barrel. This is comparable with a moderate retail sales tax of not more than 10 per cent.
2. That the excise tax on natural wine be placed at 40 cents per gallon.
3. That the excise tax on spirits be placed at $3.00 per proof gallon as an initial measure.
4. That the excise taxes upon other alcoholic beverages be rationally related to the above rates with reference to their alcoholic content, price, undesirability of consumption and luxury-use factors, as shown in the accompanying table.
5. That the manufacturers' license tax be relatively small, not in excess of $2,000.[5]
6. That every manufacturer pay, in addition to the license and excise levies, a special liquor profits tax based either on net income or on excess profits. If the profits tax is levied on net income, we suggest a rate of 50 per cent for the time being. This rate reflects the equal concern of the manufacturer and the public in the conduct of the enterprise.

---

eral Tax Systems," by Beulah Bailey, pp. 14-16.

Haig, Robert M. "The Coordination of the Federal and State Tax Systems." (Bulletin of the National Tax Association, XVIII: 66-74, December, 1932.) Address delivered before the 25th Annual Conference on Taxation, September 14, 1932.

Heer, Clarence. "The Elimination of Tax Conflicts; a preliminary canvass of suggested plans of action." Memorandum submitted to the Interstate Commission on Conflicting Taxation. 29 pp. mimeographed.

Mills, Ogden. "Financial Relations of the Federal, and State Governments." (Bulletin of the National Tax Association, XVII: 224-231, May, 1932.) Address delivered before the Bar Association of New York.

Seligman, E.R.A. "The Fiscal Outlook and the Coördination of Public Revenues." (*Political Science Quarterly*, XLVIII: 1-22, March, 1933.)

United States Congress, House Committee on Ways and Means. "Double Taxation; preliminary report of a sub-committee relative to federal and state taxation and duplication therein."

[5] We do not believe that a high license tax should be used as a method of excluding people from entering the business. This should be accomplished through the refusal to issue licenses except where "public convenience and necessity" demand it, and through manufacturing quotas established in accordance with the National Recovery Act.

7. That the excise tax on ethyl alcohol for industrial purposes remain at $1.10 per gallon.

These rates, particularly the rate upon spirits, are suggested as initial rates to be enforced during the period of transition while the organized bootlegging system is being driven out of business. How long this period will last we have no longer an outstanding menace, we anticipate that higher tax rates will be socially desirable.

Retail Tax Rates

A state which creates an Alcohol Control Authority need levy no taxes upon beverages. It will take its revenue in the form of profits included in retail prices, without encumbering itself with special tax administration in addition. However, if a state adopts the license system or any other system of private sale of liquor, taxes will be necessary. For such states we recommend that the liquor sellers' tax consist of two elements: one, a small flat license not to exceed approximately $250 per year; two, an excess profits or an income tax to be computed after all other tax payments. This low license fee will eliminate one motive for sales stimulation which was prevalent in many cities under the high license system. The profits tax will generally rest on the dealer, not on the consumer. If net income is taken as a base, we suggest 50 per cent as the appropriate rate for the reasons outlined above in connection with the manufacturers' profits tax.

We are convinced that all liquor taxes within a state should be administered by the state. There should be no additional local liquor taxes or licenses. It may be desirable for the state to share the yield of the taxes with the local units of government as has been done with various taxes in New York State for many years. This is, however, a matter which must be settled in each state on the basis of a consideration of the entire revenue system for state and local government.

Disposition of Revenues

In levying these taxes, no beneficial interests in liquor revenues

SUGGESTED METHOD OF COMPUTATION OF LIQUOR TAXES

ILLUSTRATIVE RATES PER GALLON

Beverages	Range of Alcoholic Content (by Volume)	Tax Levied in Proportion to Alcoholic Content	Tax Levied in Proportion to Production Cost	Tax Levied to Discourage Consumption	Tax Levied to Reach Luxury Consumption	Total Tax per Gallon Suggested
(1)	(2) %	(3) $	(4) $	(5) $	(6) $	(7) $
Beer...............	0 to 4	0.10	None	None	None	0.10
Strong Beer......	4 to 8	.20	None	.05	.05	.30
Wine	6 to 14	.30	.05	None	.05	.40
Sparkling Wine....	7 to 13	.30	.25	.45	2.00	3.00
Fortified wine	14 to 24	.50	.10	.30	.10	1.00
Liqueur ....Approx. 40		1.00	.40	.30	1.30	3.00
Whiskey.............Approx. 50		1.25	.05	1.45	.25	3.00

Note: This table explains the method of arriving at the interrelation of tax rates upon different kinds of beverages. The percentages in Column (2) are by volume, e.g., beer at 3.2 per cent by weight is the same as beer at 4.0 by volume. In this table we use volume because volume should be the measure used in taxation. In column (3) beer is set at 10 cent per gallon, approximately 10 per cent of the retail price. The remaining taxes in Column (3) are in mathematical proportion to the alcoholic content of each beverage. In Column (4), starting with wine at 5 cents per gallon, the levies suggested are in mathematical proportion to the average manufacturing cost of the beverages. In Column (5) whiskey is penalized three times the manufacturing cost, while the remaining heavy beverages are scaled in proportion arbitrarily on the basis of experience. In Column (6) the ratio is arbitrary with the luxury tax on sparkling wine, including champagne, at twice the cost of manufacture. Column (7) is a summation of Columns (3) to (6) inclusive.

should be created. All revenue should go into the general fund and should not be designated or earmarked for charities, hospitals, old-age pensions, etc. To weigh the needs for education, for example, against the requirements for the control of the alcohol traffic is impossible. It would provoke bitter controversy and confuse unrelated governmental problems. Moreover, when particular governmental activities are made dependent upon particular revenues, changes in the tax rates, and therefore in the yield, which might be extremely desirable as social measures, can be made only with the greatest difficulty, if at all, because of the effect of such changes on wholly unrelated enterprises.[7]

CONCLUSION

The development of a proper system for taxing alcoholic beverages is one of the most important and difficult problems placed before the nation and the states by the repeal of the Eighteenth Amendment. The effort to clear the land of the illicit liquor business and to set up reasonable and effective control can be immeasurably hindered or greatly advanced by the kind of tax system now to be established. The temptation to load on to the liquor trade all our governmental deficits should be resisted at all costs, for high taxes will produce high prices and will thus make inevitable the continuance of the moonshiner, the bootlegger and the whole system of corruption.

Tax rates upon the liquor trade should be viewed as a whole, and the objective of taxation should be neither revenue, primarily, nor punishment, but social regulation. As a means of limiting consumption, the price of beverages of high alcoholic content may be considerably increased through taxes as soon as, but not before, the illicit trade is well under control.

To make liquor taxes simple, effective and consistent, all manufacturers' taxes should be levied exclusively by the federal government and correlated with import duties. All retail taxes or licenses

---

[7] See *ante* p. 48.

should be levied by the states. There should be no local levies. The federal government might well distribute part of the manufacturers' taxes back to the states, while the states might hand part of the license fees and profits taxes back to the communities.

To avoid shifting the entire tax burden to the consumer, the principle of profits taxation should be applied to both the manufacturers and the distributors of alcoholic beverages through the levy of a special liquor profits tax.

The tax rates applied to the various kinds of alcoholic beverages should be established upon a rational basis by varying the tax rate per gallon with relation to the alcoholic content, the price, the undesirability of consumption and luxury use.   .

In harmony with these suggestions, we present a simple and rational schedule of taxes to be levied by the federal government and by the states in coöperation. The basic excise rates are $3.00 a barrel for 3.2 per cent beer, 40 cents a gallon for natural wine, and $3.00 a gallon for standard 100 proof spirits. In order that there may be no misunderstanding with regard to these proposals, we wish to repeat that these are submitted as initial tax rates to be modified in the future to meet changing conditions. It is estimated that these taxes will produce, together with the profits taxes suggested, approximately $700,000,000 a year.

Revenues from liquor taxes or licenses should not be earmarked for special purposes, such as schools, old-age pensions, hospitals and charities. The revenues should go directly into the general funds.

Although liquor prices are influenced by many factors other than taxes, it seems to us that the tax program which we have suggested will make possible a reasonable price level for alcoholic beverages. The prices for beer will probably be slightly reduced by the reduction of excise taxes and of flat licenses and the reliance on profits taxes which cannot normally be passed on to the consumer. Ordinary wine could be merchandised from $1.50 to $2.50 a gallon. Whiskey, gin and other spirits would probably sell at $1.50 and up per quart. With reasonably efficient law enforcement these prices will, we believe, make it unprofitable and difficult for organized bootlegging to continue. Though the probable price for spirits is, in our judgment, lower than it ultimately should be from the standpoint of limitation of consumption, this can be corrected by increasing the tax rates as soon as the illicit traffic has been substantially eliminated. Eventually there may be a greater differential between the beverages of low alcoholic content and those of high content.

From the standpoint of social justice the plan here recommended is clearly a marked step in advance. It lightens the taxes which fall on those with little income and through its profits tax features reaches a large new tax-paying capacity. The suggested plan rests less heavily on regressive consumption taxes and more heavily on profits taxes. At a time like the present when the country is endeavoring to increase the total share of the national income going to the lower income groups, it would seem rational to make our taxes consistent with this objective.

We are convinced that the application of these principles of taxation is essential to the successful handling of the new problems created by the repeal of the Eighteenth Amendment.

Chapter Eight

EDUCATION

So FAR IN OUR REPORT WE HAVE BEEN DISCUSSING VARIOUS TYPES OF legislative arrangements. We have been trying to find a realistic answer to this question: What defenses shall the law set up to guard society against the abuses of alcohol? But we have no illusions as to the complete success of any legal system. In our opinion there is no "solution" of the liquor problem-if by "solution" is meant some system or scheme which will be a short cut to virtue. No wave of the legislative wand can accomplish what all the saints and sages have failed to achieve in a score of centuries. While law can be of assistance,—and some laws are much more effective than others,— alcoholic indulgence is too deeply rooted in human nature to be dug out by summary process. The "solution" fetish has in the past been mischievous because it has turned our eyes toward an alluring vision, and we have too often been blind to the prosaic necessities and slower process involved in the word "education."

The Need for Education

That there is need for education in relation to the problem of alcohol will scarcely be doubted by anyone who considers the nature of the age in which we are now living. A century ago, in the dominate agricultural civilization of America, the consequences of alcoholic excess were limited largely to the victim himself, to the members of his family and to his more immediate associates. Today we are living in a machine age. The railroad engine, the truck, the automobile, the airplane, are the symbols of a new pace and tempo—the instruments by which our modern society expresses itself in

85

terms of speed. Indeed, the whole economic and industrial structure of our social order is held together by machinery,—machinery that requires cool heads and steady nerves to run it,—delicately adjusted, interlocked machinery, capable, if mishandled, of wrecking the social system itself and scattering death and suffering in wide circles.

This conception of the evils of intemperance in a machine age was alive in America long before the advent of prohibition. As early as 1899 the famous Rule G was in operation on every Class 1 railroad:

> The use of intoxicants by employees while on duty is prohibited; their use, or the frequenting of places where they are sold, is sufficient cause for dismissal.

That rule was not written by fanatics or by moralists. It was written by engineers in the interest of human safety. By the same token every automobile today is an argument against liquor; every new mechanical invention is a plea for temperance. It is this point of view that gives rise to apprehension among thoughtful people everywhere as they face a new era of liquor control, with the machine process fastening itself more securely each year on all the details of human life. Never was there a greater need for temperate habit and self-control. Never was the necessity for education so compelling.

What is Meant by Education

We are conscious, of course, that education is a much-abused term and that all too frequently it is employed as a charm by which miracles can be wrought. The public mind is tempted to fall back upon it when quicker approaches are blocked, and, like legislation, it becomes in popular imagination a final solution rather than a working method. Moreover, when we think of education, we are inclined to think almost exclusively in terms of the school. In relation to the problem of alcohol, for example, we think of the part that formal and systematized instruction can play in the development of temperate habits.

This however is a narrow and inadequate conception. As a matter of fact, the schools alone can accomplish little in modifying or stabilizing the habits of the individual. Other factors, far more potent, must be linked up in the process. There is always a temptation to impose upon the school system as a single agency responsibilities heavier than it can possibly meet. That it can equip its students with accurate, unbiased knowledge concerning the different aspects of their personal and social relationships is admitted. That it can do something in the way of making them balanced, wholesome human beings is also true. But it cannot compete with the influences nor successfully oppose the tendencies of other and stronger agencies of social control.

What are these other agencies that normally are stronger than the conventional educational process? What formative influences other than the school have to be considered? First and foremost, it seems to us, comes the general social situation in which a child grows up. With all the local differences that exist throughout the United States, there is a certain attitude toward life that may be characterized as American in that it differs from the English attitude or the German or the French or any other. This vague but indisputable social pressure upon the growing individual is well-nigh irresistible. This is the first, the most general and the most common element in the process of education.

There is a second influence of wide but more limited character, namely, the influence of the immediate environment in which the child grows up. The general spirit or attitude pertaining to American life which impresses itself upon American children and adults is modified by certain influences due to the particular characteristics of the narrower group to which the individual belongs. The standards and manners of the circle in which he moves, his intimate associations-social, religious or otherwise: these factors sway and shape his thinking and conduct.

There is a third influence of wider, varying potency, but of tremendous importance, namely, that smaller but intensely interested group, the family.

The mother, father, brothers and sisters who live under one roof make up a unit, from the influence of which it is extremely difficult for an individual to escape. The standards and ideals of this unit, its capacity to lead and persuade, constitute, therefore, a third contribution factor to the education of the growing human being.

These considerations obviously apply to the problem of temperance. Whether a country is to be dry or moist or wet will depend in the first instance on the general attitude of the vast majority of the adult persons of whom it is made up. As far as the individual is concerned, however, this attitude can be modified for better or for worse, first, by the prevailing tone of the social circle in which he grows up and, second, by the influences that surround him at home. In molding the individual toward indulgence or abstinence or moderation, these two groups with which he is most intimately connected may either confirm or obliterate the educational impact of society at large, just as one of these groups may confirm or obliterate the influence of the other.

When, therefore, we look to "education" for help in relation to temperance, let us not suppose that "education" is solely a matter of going to school. Far more important in the development of rational and balanced living are those subtle and intangible factors which constitute the tone and quality of the nation, the community and the home. As with every other problem that relates to conduct, temperance in the long run will come, not by summary process or legislative decree, nor by formal instruction in the school, but only as our entire American culture becomes civilized and the level of social standards and desires is raised.

The Place of the School

In spite of the fact that the school is less important than other agencies affecting the individual, it still has a significant part to play. At this point, however, difficulties are immediately encountered. What shall the school teach? What shall be the goal of its instruction? Too often, when a specific problem appears on the horizon, the school is enlisted and instruction is begun with little consideration of the question whether there is a system of ideas or a code of behavior so generally accepted that the country or the locality is willing to have itself indoctrinated with it. In other words, the wheels of the educational process are set in motion before there is any agreement as to objective and aim.

This tendency has been particularly evident in regard to the problem of alcohol. Today every state in the Union, with the exception of Wyoming and Arizona, requires compulsory public school temperance instruction. In general, the statutes prescribe that in all schools supported wholly or in part by public funds specific and graduated courses in hygiene shall be given for designated periods with special reference to the effects of alcohol upon the human system. In some states teachers have been dismissed and appropriations withheld if the anti-alcohol subjects are not taught as required by law. In other states certificates have been denied until teachers pass satisfactory examinations in hygiene, including the effects of alcohol on character and health. Thirteen states have set aside one day of each year, known in the schools as Temperance Day, during which exercises are held on the general subject of the effect and influence of drinking habits.

The difficulty with all this activity is its lack of concrete objective. What is meant by "temperance teaching"? Does one mean moderation in the use of alcoholic beverages, or is total abstinence the aim? As a matter of fact, the dry forces have interpreted compulsory temperance instruction in terms of total abstinence while the anti-drys have thought of it as meaning the teaching of moderation. Thus the conflict between wets and drys in the political field has been reflected in the educational field; and the type and degree of instruction in a given locality have too often been determined by whether one group or the other was in the ascendancy.

This uncertainty, this lack of definition, is undoubtedly one of the reasons why the educational program with reference to temperance has, in many states, seemed so inadequate. In localities where dry sentiment is pronounced, the instruction has often been given with the aid of biased and unscientific textbooks by teachers whose methods have been largely limited to moralizing and propaganda. On the other hand, in more or less wet districts, the instruction has frequently been perfunctory and the teachers indifferent and hostile.

Lack of Knowledge in Temperance Education

Temperance education, like all education, has been impeded not only by lack of aim, but by lack of knowledge. It is easy to say that only those facts should be taught which have been scientifically as-certained. But as between the advocates of abstinence and the advo-cates of temperance, what agreement is there in relation to any body of facts scientifically ascertained? Authorities are quoted by both sides, and each bases its case on an appeal to science. Indeed, one of the discouraging aspects of the liquor debate of the last decade has been the use of scientific and pseudo-scientific terminology as a weapon of war. All the branches of learning from physiology to aesthetics and from sociology to ethics have been conscripted for service, not in a detached and disinterested search for truth, but as a means of propaganda. In the heat of the controversy any kind of fact has served as a weapon, and these "facts" have been fed out far too indiscriminately to the children in the school system.

A Possible New Approach

It is no part of the business of the authors of this volume to outline a course of education in the school sense of the term. That must be left to the intelligence of the schoolmen themselves. It is our concern, however, to point out that just as the schools now endeavor to give systematic, reliable and unbiased instruction in the field of dietetics or clothing, for example, so they may fairly be asked to per-form the same service in reference to the health and social aspects of alcohol. But just as in America the public schools are forbidden to take a biased attitude in respect to politics or religion, so they ought to refrain from taking a biased or prejudiced attitude toward any other subject related to personal conduct or manners.

The possibility of a new approach through the schools is elab-

---

[1] Published in 1930. (Second printing July, 1931). Dr. Thomas D. Wood served as the Chairman.

orated in a recent report on health problems in education, issued by joint committees of the National Education Association and the American Medical Association, with the coöperation of the Technical Committee of Twenty-Seven.[1] We have no space to quote at length from this report, but the following paragraphs are significant:

The instruction concerning alcohol, tobacco, and other narcotics should be, in the main, a part of the general work in training to personal health habits and to promotion of community health and welfare. The keynote should be, "Teach by facts and illustration; not by exhortation."

Ideally, the instruction should be positive and demonstrative. Practically, the persistence of erroneous traditional beliefs about these substances, especially about alcohol, makes necessary concrete knowledge of their nature and effect as reason for practicing sobriety.

The choice of material, therefore, involves: (1) Recognition of the individual and community advantages resulting from sobriety; (2) correction of current fallacies as to the nature and effects of these substances in which much of their use finds excuse; (3) definite knowledge of modern scientific experiments and observations on this subject; (4) the application of this information to practical conditions of modern life in meeting individual and community problems. There are, for example, industrial and transportation conditions now which make the use of alcoholic liquors very much more dangerous in their results than was the case a century ago. The physiological lesson should be deftly interwoven with the concrete instruction.

Facts taught should be graded to meet the interest and psychological development of pupils. Motivation may be given through the appeal to desire for fitness for sports, efficiency in play and work, vigorous health, safety, service of others, character qualities such as self-control, kindness, sportsmanship, self-reliance, duty, reliability, truth, good workmanship, coöperation, loyalty. Incidental training may be given in connection with or through arithmetic, language, history, geography, biography, English, drawing, projects. Much of this information will find its way through the children back into the home, and if constructively developed, will often react on the home environment favorably to the child's physical, mental, and moral development.

In this outline positive ideals around which physical facts may be taught are suggested solely as a guide to the teacher, but are never to be made a basis for "moralizing." The success of this training will depend in no small degree upon leading young people to discover for themselves from the facts that sobriety has a value which makes it desirable to them in promoting activities or ideals in which they have interest.

Factors in the New Approach

If any such educational program is to be developed, it seems to us that there are a few principles which require emphasis:

1. The need for research is paramount. We must have the facts about the effects of alcohol on the human system, facts which scientists of accepted standing can support. It is to be hoped that with the passing of the Eighteenth Amendment the heated spirit of controversy will subside, and objective consideration will take its place. There are many gaps in our knowledge at the present moment, and medicine and physiology have much to learn. In the meantime efforts should be made to bring together in tangible form the facts which have thus far been ascertained, and nothing should be taught upon which the leading authorities in medical science are in disagreement. Controversial issues, such as the effect of alcohol on heredity, can be explained and presented from the different points of view now held by various authorities. School textbooks should have constant and searching revision in these matters as in all others that require change through new gains in knowledge. Wherever exaggerated statements regarding the effects of alcohol are found, they should be eliminated in order to make possible the objective teaching of what is known to be true.

2. Not only do we need research so that facts can displace opinion and superstition, but we need clear, unprejudiced dissemination of facts. This requires a tolerant spirit, and tolerance in education, free from the bias of preconceived objectives, is perhaps difficult to achieve. But it is distinctly within the range of possibility to promote understanding of facts to a point where common knowledge supports a steadily improving national ideal.

3. Whatever line temperance instruction may take, its chief emphasis, if it is to capture this younger generation, should be on life and health and not on disease and death. It should be constructive and not negative. The necessity of keeping fit for work and sport is a far more effective appeal than moral homilies. Our young people cannot be browbeaten into righteousness or frightened into good be-

havior. They are alert to detect exaggeration, and they are not moved by sanctimonious exhortation. It is this kind of approach which has too often made temperance teaching in the past what on well-known educator called a "pedagogical monstrosity." The only effective appeal today is an appeal not to fear or prejudice but to intelligence.

Adult Education

If systematic temperance education is to be truly effective, it must be pushed beyond the limits of the schoolroom. It is at this point that a significant opportunity is developing in the new era which we are now entering. With the old wet and dry controversy out of the way, the argument of sobriety, for temperate living, for a clean and orderly country can be made in a manner that will stir the nation. It is possible that this activity could be assisted through the State Boards of Education and other public bodies; but here is a field well adapted to private societies—Chambers of Commerce, Parent-Teacher Associations, civic agencies, churches, as well as organizations specially created for this purpose.

It is possible that a new society for temperance, set up perhaps on a national basis and divorced from old groups and methods that have outlived their usefulness, might be of genuine service. Such an organization could focus specialized attention on the problem and could bring together behind intelligent programs men and women interested in the maintenance of a sober country, and determined that the legalized return of alcohol shall mark the beginning of real temperance.

Conclusion

In an earlier section of this chapter we spoke of a distinct American atmosphere or attitude and the social pressure it exerts upon the growing individual. What is needed in this country is a national ideal, a public will, a deep desire to eradicate the evils of alcoholic excess.

In a number of countries which we have investigated, this spirit of determination is at work. In England, for example, in spite of the natural handicaps of a license system, there is a definite, conscious effort toward the attainment of temperance. Similarly throughout Scandinavia, substantial reduction in the consumption of spirits has been effected by health education, by the promotion of sports, and by the purposeful leadership of public spirited men. In Russia, a nation-wide campaign for temperance is now in process. Indeed with the Russians, the fight for temperance has been thrown into terms of a vast symbol. Vodka, an enemy of the people, is battling at their gates. Guards are stationed in every home, school and factory. Alcoholic clinics and psychiatric wards as well as posters and lectures, are the weapons employed. From White Russia to Siberia, from the Black Sea to the Baltic, the voice of temperance leadership is heard. It is a spirit that is reflected in the daily life of the people and finds expression in a thousand forms. As a consequence, in Russia the forces of intemperance are in retreat.

It may be said that conditions abroad are utterly different from those in the United States, and the point, of course, is true. But here are examples of what can be done by the power of a national determination to check and minimize the evils of intemperance. It is this kind of ideal, this united front against a common danger, that could change age-old attitudes toward liquor and give temperance and sobriety a sure foothold in our Twentieth Century civilization.

Chapter Nine

TOWARD CONTROL

LAW AND EDUCATION ARE TWIN PILLARS OF THE SOCIAL ORDER. IN RESPECT to most human problems, the hope of the future lies in laws soundly conceived and well administered and in an educational process rooted in self-discipline and self-control.

But this is an easy generalization and it does not answer the legitimate apprehension with which the thoughtful people of this country face a new attempt at liquor regulation. After a thirteen-year trial of national prohibition, the pendulum has swung violently toward toleration. The influence of this new attitude is bound to affect the legislation in each of the forty-eight states. But toleration, unless rigidly guarded, means the inevitable return of evils which those of us whose memories run back a quarter of a century do not like to recall. It was only twenty years ago that the saloon, backed by the brewers and the distillers, had a throttle grip on local and state government alike, a grip which it maintained by systematic corruption. As late as 1915 the organized liquor traffic tried to blacklist forty-nine American firms, including railroads and manufacturing concerns, which in the interests of efficiency had forbidden their employees the use of intoxicants while on duty. It is scarcely an exaggeration to say that the liquor business, as organized before prohibition, stood for everything that decency was opposed to and fought everything that decency desired. That there were individuals here and there in both the retail and the wholesale business who were respectable and socially responsible citizens must, of course, be admitted. But their voices were unheard in the clamor of the trade for increased profits. The belief that national prohibition was "put over" by fanatical moralists is a common fallacy. In large measure the Eighteenth Amendment was the final result of angry public re-action, accumulating over a long period of years, against a system that debauched personal character, corrupted public life and defined control.

The younger generation, perhaps, has no vivid recollection of this old regime, but the older generation remembers it; and the warn-ing we would pass to those who must handle the responsibility in the future is based on memories of a nation fighting for temperate standards against a lawless trade.

The Basis of our Recommendations

It is because we realize so keenly the possibilities of abuse in-volved in the present swing toward toleration that we have come to the conclusions embodied in this report. We do not favor the license system, because it seems to us inadequate to control the abuses of strong alcoholic beverages. It does not stop the gap from which most of the evils flow. We are not impressed with the possibilities of state-wide bone-dry prohibition, not because in theory it is too drastic, but because in practice it does not work. Restrictive laws which cannot be enforced achieve success only on paper. More than that, they defeat their fundamental purpose. Our recommendation in regard to the liberalization of the control of light beers and wines may seem to some too extreme a concession to wet sentiment. We are convinced, however, that without this degree of liberalization there is no escape from the bootlegger and but little hope for real temperance. On the other hand, our recommendation in regard to state control of the sale of stronger alcoholic beverages may appear to some too bold and idealistic an experiment in governmental operation. But we firmly believe that any system of control which does not attack the pri-vate profit motive in the retail sale of spirits is merely touching the problem at its fringe. Unless we eliminate the incentive behind the stimulation of sale, we have not dug to the root of the difficulty, and the weeds of abuse will thrive no matter how we hack at the tops.

Other Experiments Desirable

In making this recommendation for a State Authority we do not wish to appear dogmatic or intolerant of other control devices that may be suggested. In a country as large as ours, with so great a variety of local conditions, there is room for many types of experiment. Indeed, the forty-eight states will constitute a social science laboratory in which different ideas and methods can be tested, and the exchange of experience will be infinitely valuable for the future.

It is perhaps unnecessary to make the point that no inherent virtue resides in any given type of administrative mechanism. Assuming that the objectives of the regulatory system are reasonably satisfactory to the community, it is the men in charge of the machinery who determine failure or success. In the last analysis, integrity and intelligence are of far greater importance than administrative device. The conclusion of the Committee of Fifty in 1903, at the close of its ten-year survey of the liquor problem, is as true today as it was thirty years ago: "That law is best which is best administered."

At the same time, it is possible to set up a system of control in which administrative intelligence and integrity are not confronted at the beginning with impossible obstacles. It is precisely this reasoning that leads us to prefer the State Authority system. Instead of being pitted at the start against a business that is looking for maximum profits at any cost, the administrators of such a system could develop their policies protected for the hazard of an immediate and insidious warfare. Plenty of enemies would remain to be fought, but among them would not be the one that in America at least has upset every governmental attempt in a hundred years that looked toward temperance and moderation, i.e., a hungry liquor traffic with an eye only to larger profits.

No System Final

A concluding word remains to be said: No recommendations which we or anyone else could make carry with them an element of finality. The only service that law can render is to give effect to the necessities and ideals of a given time and place, and necessities and ideals cannot escape the processes of change. We need to be on our guard against any system of control that has outlived its usefulness of that no longer represents the prevalent ideas and attitudes of the community. Our legal prescriptions and formulas must be living conceptions, capable of growing as we grow. For law is itself a social phenomenon and has no meaning apart from the uses and necessities from which it springs.

The point is important because of all public questions the liquor question swings its pendulum through the widest arc. The opinion of this decade is not likely to be the opinion of the next; and in their attempt to find a method of regulation which meets the contemporary mood and attitude, lawmakers are often sorely perplexed. At the moment this country has turned in strong reaction against the restrictions of a national prohibition system. Forty-eight states are attempting to set up a new method of control. In the last analysis, there is but one fundamental rule to be followed—and all other rules are corollaries: If the new system is not rooted in what the people of each state sincerely desire at this moment, it makes no difference how logical and complete it may appear as a statute—it cannot succeed.

But, unless we mistake the desire and temper of public opinion, there is no disposition to allow the return of old evils. A new spirit is in the air—a new belief in the power of human intelligence to plan a social order in the interests of a saner and more balanced life. It is this revived faith, this impatience with abuses which have so long seemed inevitable, this willingness to experiment, that constitute the hope of the new era.

APPENDICES

AMERICAN LAWS
AND CONSTITUTIONAL PROVISIONS

WILSON ORIGINAL PACKAGES ACT

Act of August 8, 1890, c. 728 (26 Stat. 313)

All fermented, distilled, or other intoxicating liquors or liquids transported into any State or Territory or remaining therein for use, consumption, sale or storage therein, shall upon arrival in such State or Territory be subject to the operation and effect of the laws of such State or Territory enacted in the exercise of its police powers, to the same extent and in the same manner as though such liquids or liquors had been produced in such State or Territory, and shall not be exempt therefrom by reason of being introduced therein in original packages or otherwise.

WEBB-KENYON ACT

Act of March 1, 1913, c. 90 (37 Stat. 699)

*(The Webb Bill—An Act divesting intoxicating liquors of their
interstate charters in certain cases)*

The shipment or transportation, in any manner or by any means whatsoever, of any spirituous, vinous, malted, fermented, or other intoxicating liquor of any kind, from one State, Territory or District of the United States, or place noncontiguous to but subject to the jurisdiction thereof, into any other State, Territory, or District of the United States, or place noncontiguous to but subject to the jurisdiction thereof, or from any foreign country into any State, Territory, or District of the United States, or place noncontiguous to but subject to the jurisdiction thereof, which said spirituous, vinous, malted, fermented, or other intoxicating liquor is intended, by any person interested therein, to be received, possessed, sold, or in any manner used, either in the original package or otherwise, in violation of any law of such State, Territory, or District of the United States, or place noncontiguous to but subject to the jurisdiction thereof, is hereby prohibited.

REED AMENDMENT

Act of March 3, 1917, c. 162, Sec. 5, (39 Stat. 1069)
Act of March 4, 1917, c. 192, (39 Stat. 1202)
Act of February 24, 1919, c. 18, Sec. 1407, (40 Stat. 1151)

Whoever shall order, purchase, or cause intoxicating liquors to be transported in interstate commerce, except for scientific, sacramental, medicinal, and mechanical purposes, into any State or Territory the laws of which State or Territory prohibit the manufacture or sale therein of intoxicating liquors for beverage purposes shall be fined not more than $1,000 or imprisoned not more than six months, or both; Provided, That nothing herein shall authorize the shipment of liquor into any State contrary to the laws of such State; Provided further, That the provisions of this section are made applicable to the District of Columbia....

No letter, postal card, circular, newspaper, pamphlet, or publication of any kind containing any advertisement of spirituous, vinous, malted, fermented, or other intoxicating liquors of any kind, or containing a solicitation of an order or orders for said liquors, or any of them, shall be deposited in or carried by the mails of the United States, or be delivered by any postmaster or letter carrier, when addressed or directed to any person, firm, corporation, or association, or other addressee, at any place or point in any State or Territory of the United States, or the District of Columbia, at which it is by the law in force in the State or Territory or the District of Columbia at that time unlawful to advertise or solicit orders for such liquors, or any of them, respectively. If the publisher of any newspaper or other publication or the agent of such publisher, or if any dealer in such liquors or his agent, shall knowingly deposit, or cause to be deposited, or shall knowingly send or cause to be sent, anything to be conveyed or delivered by mail in violation of the provisions of this section, or shall knowingly deliver or cause to be delivered by mail anything herein forbidden to be carried by mail, shall be fined not more than $1,000 or imprisoned not more than six months, or both; and for any subsequent offense shall be imprisoned not more than one year. Any person violating any provision of this section may be tried and punished, either in the district in which the unlawful matter or publication was mailed or to which it was carried by mail for delivery, according to direction thereon, or in which it was caused to be delivered by mail to the person to whom it was addressed. The Postmaster General is hereby authorized and directed to make public from time to time in suitable bulletins or public notices the names of States in which it is unlawful to advertise or solicit orders for such liquors.

EIGHTEENTH AMENDMENT

(Liquor Prohibition)

1.   After one year from the ratification of this article the manufacture, sale, or transportation of intoxicating liquors within, the importation thereof into, or the exportation thereof from the United States and all territory subject to the jurisdiction thereof for beverage purposes is hereby prohibited.

2.   The Congress and the several States shall have concurrent power to enforce this article by appropriate legislation.

3.   This article shall be inoperative unless it shall have been ratified as an amendment to the Constitution by the Legislatures of the several States, as provided in the Constitution, within seven years from the date of the submission hereof to the States by the Congress.

Put into effect January 16, 1920

SUMMARY OF THE VOLSTEAD ACT

National Prohibition Act of October 28, 1919, c. 85, Sec. I (41 Stat. 305)

The word "liquor" as used in the law includes alcohol, brandy, whiskey, rum, gin, beer, ale, porter, and wine, or other beverages containing one half of one percent or more of alcohol. All persons are forbidden to manufacture, sell, barter, transport, import, export, deliver, furnish or possess any intoxicating liquor except under the provisions of the act. The law permits under regulation denatured alcohol and denatured rum; medicinal preparations made according to regular formulas, patent medicines, toilet articles, antiseptic preparations, flavoring extracts and syrups, provided these are unfit for beverage uses; vinegar and sweet cider. In the manufacture of cereal beverages, the production of high-proof beer is permitted as a part of the process but it must be de-alcoholized before offered for sale. Liquor for non-beverage purposes and sacramental wine may be manufactured, etc., under certain regulations. Manufacturers of exempt articles may purchase and keep liquor for such purposes under certain conditions, but may not sell it or use it, except as ingredients of the articles manufactured. No more alcohol may be used in articles which may be used as beverages than the necessary amount for solution of certain elements and for preservation of the articles.

No one may manufacture, etc., liquor without a permit, but liquor prescribed by a physician may be bought without a permit. A person conducting a bona fide hospital or sanatorium for alcoholics may under certain regulations purchase and use liquor for the treatment of patients under physician's direction.

Anyone having a permit to manufacture, etc., wine for sacramental purposes may sell it only to a rabbi, minister, priest, or officer authorized by a congregation on special application.

Only licensed active physicians holding permits may prescribe liquor and then only if they believe that the use of liquor as medicine by the person is necessary.

Under the 1921 amendment [Nov. 23, 1921, c. 134, Sec. 2 (42 Stat. 222)] physicians may prescribe only spirituous and vinous liquor but may not prescribe for one person more than a pint of spirituous liquors or a quart of wine within ten days.

Various types of records are prescribed for manufacturers, wholesale and retail druggists and common carriers.

It is unlawful for a person to ship liquor without notifying the carrier of the contents of the package; for the carrier to accept for shipment a package of liquor unless certain information appears on the label; to receive, ship or transport a package of liquor bearing false statements; to give carrier an order for delivery of liquor to a person who has no right to receive it; to advertise in any way liquor, its manufacture or sale or where it may be secured, except that manufacturers or wholesale druggists holding permits may furnish price lists and advertise in trade journals, and that the provision is not to apply to foreign newspapers mailed to this country; to advertise, manufacture, sell or possess any utensil, recipe, etc., for the unlawful manufacture of liquor; to solicit or permit one's employees to solicit orders for liquor or information as to how it may be secured.

Anyone injured by an intoxicated person shall have right of action for damages against the person who sold the liquor unlawfully to the intoxicated person.

Possession of liquor in one's private dwelling only for the personal consumption of the owner, his family and bona fide guests is legal if obtained lawfully prior to the effective date of the Eighteenth Amendment to the Constitution.

A good deal of misunderstanding has arisen over the exemptions made in the interest of home manufacture and consumption of liquor. "Non-intoxicating cider and fruit juices" may be manufactured, exclusively for use in the home; and here the Bureau of Prohibition interprets the work "non-intoxicating" to mean non-intoxicating in fact without reference to an exact percentage of alcoholic content. Fruit juices, except cider, thus manufactured are subject to tax if they exceed one-half of one per cent in alcoholic content under the revenue laws.

SUMMARY OF THE JONES LAW

Act of March 2, 1929, c. 473, Sec. I (45 Stat. 1446)

Wherever a penalty or penalties are prescribed in a criminal prosecution by the National Prohibition Act, as amended and supplemented, for the illegal manufacture, sale, transportation, importation or exportation of intoxicating liquor, as defined by Section I, Title II, of the National Prohibition Act, the penalty imposed for each such offense shall be a fine not to exceed $10,000 or imprisonment not to exceed five years, or both; Provided, That it is the intent of Congress that the court, in imposing sentence hereunder, should discriminate between casual or slight violations and habitual sales of intoxicating liquor, or attempts to commercialize violations of the law.

Section 2. This act shall not repeal nor eliminate any minimum penalty for the first or any subsequent offense now provided by the said National Prohibition Act.

•   •   •   •   •   •   •   •

This Jones Act was modified by the Stibbs Law passed January 15, 1931 (c. 29, 46 Stat. 1036), to make petty offenders, selling or manufacturing or transporting not more than a gallon of liquor subject to a maximum fine of $500, instead of $10,000, and a maximum imprisonment of not more than six months instead of five years.

SUMMARY OF ACT LEGALIZING 3.2% BEER

(Cullen Beer Act)
Act of March 22, 1933, Sec. 3 (48 Stat. —)

A tax of $5 per barrel (31 gallons) is levied on all malt and vinous beverages containing one-half of one per cent, or more, of alcohol by volume, and not more than 3.2 per cent of alcohol by weight, and at a like rate for any other quantity or for the fractional parts of a barrel authorized and defined by law, to be collected under the provisions of existing law. The tax imposed by this section upon any beverage, if any tax is now imposed thereon by law is to be in lieu of such tax. This provision does not affect the internal revenue tax on beer or wine of an alcoholic content greater than 3.2 per cent by weight or less than one-half of one per cent by volume.

There is required of brewers for each brewery a federal license fee of $1,000.

Nothing in this Act is to be construed as repealing any special tax or administrative provision of the internal revenue laws applicable to malt and vinous beverages of an alcoholic content of not less than one-half of one per cent by volume and not more than 3.2

per cent by weight.

The restrictions of the Reed Amendment in regard to advertising of liquors are not to apply to malt and vinous beverages of an alcoholic content not greater than 3.2 per cent by weight.

Manufacturers must secure a permit before engaging in business, such permits to be withheld in states where such manufacture is prohibited.

Manufacturers' permits must specify a maximum alcoholic content permissible for the fermented malt or vinous liquor or fruit juice at the time of withdrawal from the factory or other disposition, which shall not be greater than 3.2 per cent by weight.

If in the process of manufacture a greater percentage of alcohol than that permitted by law is produced, the excess must, before the liquid is withdrawn from the factory, be reduced to or below the specified maximum; but such liquid may be removed and transported, under bond and under such regulations as may be prescribed, from one bonded plant or warehouse to another for the purpose of having the percentage of alcohol reduced to the maximum specified in the permit by dilution or extraction,

No tax shall be assessed or paid on spirits used in fortifying wines for the production of non-beverage alcohol.

In cases where the manufacturer is charged with manufacturing or selling for beverage purposes any beer or wine containing more than 3.2 per cent of alcohol by weight, the burden of proof shall be on such manufacturer to show that the liquid so manufactured or sold contained not more than 3.2 per cent of alcohol by weight. If a manufacturer is charged with failure to reduce the alcoholic content to or below the maximum permitted under this act, the burden of proof is likewise on him to show that the alcoholic content so manufactured or sold did not exceed the maximum specified in the permit. In any suit or proceeding involving the alcoholic content of any beverage, the reasonable expense of analysis of such beverage shall be taxed as costs in the case.

For violations of this provision the manufacturer is subject to the penalties and proceedings provided by law in the case of similar violations of the National Prohibition Act.

Interstate shipment, or importation in violation of state law, is prohibited. The fine for violation of this provision is not more then $1,000 or imprisonment for not more than six months, or both, and for any subsequent offense imprisonment for not more than one year. If any person is convicted under this section any permit issued to him shall be revoked.

TWENTY-FIRST AMENDMENT

(Repeal)

1. The Eighteenth Article of Amendment to the Constitution of the United States is hereby repealed.

2. The transportation or importation into any State, Territory or possession of the United States for delivery or use therein of intoxicating liquors, in violation of the laws thereof, is hereby prohibited.

3. This article shall be inoperative unless it shall have been ratified as an amendment to the Constitution by conventions in the several states, as provided in the Constitution, within seven years from the date of submission hereof to the States by Congress.

APPENDIX II

H O W   T H E   C A N A D I A N   P R O V I N C E S

QUEBEC

GOVERNMENT CONTROL

METHOD OF
CONTROL

A Liquor Commission appointed by the Lieutenant-Governor-in-Council consisting at present of 5 Commissioners—no fixed term. The Commission, at its own stores, makes retail sales, by the bottle, of spirituous liquor, wine, imported beer (exceeding 4% in alcohol by weight). No sales by the glass at liquor stores.

MANUFACTURE
AND
IMPORTATION

Manufacture in private hands, with strict supervision by the Commission of all breweries and distilleries. Liquor Commission alone may import.

WHOLESALE

All provincial sales by the distilleries are made only to the Commission, which supplies the government retail stores from its own warehouses. No wholesale sales of wine for consumption within the Province except to the Commission. Breweries sell beer at wholesale to different licensees (grocers, etc.).

LOCAL OPTION

Much used feature of the Liquor Act. Mail and express order purchases from Commission headquarters in Montreal and Quebec permitted in local option areas.

LICENSES

All manufacturing is under federal control and taxation, but sales come under the Commission. Breweries, hotels, taverns, cafés, clubs, restaurants, groceries, licensed by the Commission. A banquet permit is provided for. All licenses or permits good for not exceeding 1 year.

APPENDIX II

HANDLE ALCOHOLIC BEVERAGES

NEW BRUNSWICK— GOVERNMENT CONTROL	ALBERTA— GOVERNMENT CONTROL
A Liquor Control Board of 3 members appointed by the Governor-in-Council— the Chief Commissioner's appointment is for 10 years. All retail sales of spirituous liquor, imported beer and wine made by the Board in its own stores—by the bottle. No sales by the glass—no public drinking.	A liquor Board—1 Commissioner appointed by the Executive Council. No fixed period of appointment—the present Commissioner has held office since the Act was set up. All retail sales of spirituous liquor, imported beer and wine made by the Board in its own store—by the bottle. No sales by the glass of spirituous liquor—no public drinking (except beer).
The breweries are privately owned and subject to strict supervision by the Board. Liquor Control Board alone may import.	The breweries are privately owned and subject to strict supervision by the Board. No distillery in Alberta. Liquor Board alone may import.
All sales by the breweries to the Board which supplies the government retail stores from its own warehouse at Fredericton. Wholesale for shipment outside the Province by the brewers, and records of all such sales must be filed with the Board.	Alberta brewers sell wholesale direct to licensees and report sales to the Board.
Much used feature of the Liquor Act. Mail and express order purchases permitted in local option areas—shipped from head office at Fredericton.	Much used feature of the Liquor Act. Mail and express order purchases permitted in local option areas—shipped from head office at Edmonton.
No distillery and no winery in New Brunswick. Breweries subject to both federal and provincial control as to licensing and taxation. All licenses or permits good for not exceeding 1 year.	Manufacturing under federal control and taxation and subject to federal licensing. Special permits or licenses granted to druggists, physicians, hospitals, dentists, certain manufacturers, ministers, priests, etc. Brewers licensed by the Board. All licenses or permits issued for calendar year only. Banquet licenses issued subject to police approval.

QUEBEC—Cont.

PURCHASE CONDITIONS	No individual permit required.
AMOUNT ONE MAY BUY	Spirituous liquor sales limited to 1 bottle at a sale. Wine or beer sales not limited in quantity.
HOURS OF SALE	Liquor stores open from 9 a.m. to 6 p.m., Saturdays 1 p.m. (or may, if directed, remain open until 5 p.m.). Two stores each in Montreal and Quebec open until 11 p.m.; Hull, Three Rivers, Sherbrooke each has one store open until 11 p.m. Taverns open from 8 a.m. to 11 p.m. Hotels sell with meals wine and beer from 8 a.m. to 11 p.m. Taverns, liquor stores closed on church holidays, Sundays, and election days, but not on certain legal holidays such as Dominion Day, Labor Day, etc. Hotels may not sell on such days. Hotels may sell on church holidays and Sundays in Montreal and Quebec if they have 50 rooms, and in other places if they have 25 rooms, between 12 noon and 11 p.m., with meals only.
HOW BEER AND WINES ARE SOLD	Licensed breweries, both in and outside the Province sell beer direct to licensed grocers, restaurants, hotels, clubs, etc. Beer sold by the glass in licensed taverns, hotels, clubs, restaurants, railroad dining cars, vessels. In hotels, clubs and restaurants beer and wine sold only with meals. Food may be served in taverns. Wine sold only in government stores, as well as imported beer over 4% by weight.
HOW DISTILLED SPIRITS ARE SOLD	Through government stores only—by the bottle (only 1 bottle at a sale). Also by mail and express from Commission headquarters at Montreal and Quebec.
ADVERTISING	Allowed.

NEW BRUNSWICK—*Cont.*

No individual permit required.

ALBERTA—*Cont.*

A permit necessary to buy spirituous liquor and beer. Yearly fee $2.00 covering spirituous liquor and beer, also wine; $1.00 yearly fee covering beer only; single purchase permit 50 cents; non-resident permit good for 30 days $1.00.

One bottle of spirits at a sale. No restriction on beer and wine. Board may in its discretion restrict sales.

All purchases except beer entered in permit holder's permit book. No limit on spirituous liquor, wine or beer, but Board has authority to restrict sales.

From 9:30 a.m. to 5:30 p.m.—Saturdays from 9 a.m. to 5 p.m.

Beer parlor hours 7 a.m. to 10 p.m. Mon. to Fri. (9 p.m. Sat.) Hours for government stores in larger centers and mining camps, 10 a.m. to 8 p.m.; rural centers, 10 a.m. to 6 p.m. Closed Sundays, legal holidays and election days. No drinking in government stores.

Locally made beer as well as imported beer and wine, sold only at government stores.

Imported beer and wind sold only in government stores. Alberta beer also sold at government stores and through brewery warehouses maintained by the brewers, direct to individual permit holders, and to licensed beer parlors, etc. Brewers must report all sales to the Board.

Through government stores only—by the bottle, and by mail and express from head office at Fredericton.

Through government stores only—by the bottle.

Not allowed.

The board does not advertise, but manufacturers may, subject to the Board's approval.

QUEBEC—*Cont.*

PROFITS

All profits from retail sales at government stores go direct to Provincial Treasury, but substantial amounts from liquor revenues are devoted to roads, hospitals, educational purposes, etc.

TAXES EXCISE AND
CUSTOMS DUTY

Quebec breweries pay 5% tax on gross sales monthly. Outside breweries pay 5% tax on gross sales in Quebec.

Note:—For information on federal (Dominion) customs and excise taxes see p. 122.

NEW BRUNSWICK — *Cont.*

All profits from all sales at government stores go direct to Provincial Treasury.

There is no tax on beer.

Note: — For information on federal (Dominion) customs and excise taxes see p. 122.

ALBERTA — *Cont.*

All profits from retail sales at government stores go direct to Provincial Treasury.

Brewers pay a tax of 15½¢ per Imperial gal. on local sales — no tax if exported.

Note: — For information on federal (Dominion) customs and excise taxes see p. 122.

NOVA SCOTIA—
GOVERNMENT CONTROL

METHOD OF CONTROL	A Liquor Control Board of 2 members at present, appointed for 10 years by the Governor-in-Council. All retail sales of spirituous liquor, imported beer and wine made by the Board in its own stores—by the bottle. No sales by the glass—no public drinking.
MANUFACTURE AND IMPORTATION	The brewery is privately owned, subject to strict supervision by the Board. No distillery in Nova Scotia. Liquor Control Board alone may import.
WHOLESALE	Liquor Control Board has exclusive control.
LOCAL OPTION	Mail and express order purchases from head office permitted for delivery into dry areas, as determined by the Plebiscite Act of 1929.
LICENSES	All manufacturing under federal control and taxation and subject to federal licensing. Special permits granted druggists, certain manufacturers, doctors, hospitals, etc. Brewers licensed to sell to the Board. All licenses and permits good for not exceeding 1 year. Banquet licenses granted—fee $1.00.

MANITOBA— GOVERNMENT CONTROL	SASKATCHEWAN— GOVERNMENT CONTROL
A Liquor Board appointed by the Lieutenant-Governor-in-Council—3 members—no fixed term of office (present Chairman has served 10 years). All retail sales of spirituous liquor, imported beer and wine made by the Board. Sales of beer by the glass in beer parlors licensed by the Board. No sales by the glass of spirituous liquor. No public drinking in hotels or restaurants of spirituous liquor, excepting at banquets under permits or under a special permit.	A Liquor Board of 1 Commissioner at present without fixed term of office appointed by the Lieutenant-Governor-in-Council. All retail sales of spirituous liquor, imported beer and wine made by the Board in its own stores—by the bottle. No sales by the glass—no public drinking.
Manufacture in private hands, with strict supervision by the Board of all breweries and distilleries. Liquor Control Board alone may import.	Manufacture in private hands, with strict supervision by the Board of all breweries and distilleries. Liquor Control Board alone may import.
All provincial sales by the distilleries are made direct to the Board which supplies the government retail stores from its own warehouses. No wholesale of beer for consumption within the Province to other than the Board.	No wholesale of beer for consumption within the Province to other than the Board.
Much used feature of the Liquor Act. Mail and express order purchases from Board headquarters at Winnipeg permitted in local option areas.	Much used feature of the Liquor Act. Mail and express order purchases from government stores permitted in local option areas.
All manufacturing is under federal control and taxation and subject to federal licensing. The Board may grant beer, club, druggists', canteen, brewers' and distillers' licenses. Beer waiters are also licensed. All licenses or permits good for not exceeding 1 year.	Manufacturing is under federal control and taxation and subject to federal licensing. No distillery and no winery within the Province. Special permits granted to druggists, physicians, hospitals, dentists, certain manufacturers, etc. Brewers are licensed. All licenses or permits good for not exceeding 1 year.

NOVA SCOTIA—*Cont.*

PURCHASE CONDITIONS	No purchase permit required for wine and beer. Permit required for spirituous liquor. Resident individual permit fee $1.00, temporary (non-resident) individual permit fee $1.00.
AMOUNT ONE MAY BUY	The quantity of spirituous liquor, wine and beer one may buy is left to the discretion of the store manager.
HOURS OF SALE	Government stores 10 a.m. to 6 p.m. Closed Sundays, legal holidays, election days. No drinking in government stores.
HOW BEER AND WINES ARE SOLD	Through government retail stores only—by the bottle.
HOW DISTILLED SPIRITS ARE SOLD	Through government stores only—by the bottle.

MANITOBA—*Cont.*

Individual purchase permits for wine and beer and spirituous liquor $1.00 yearly fee; special temporary permit to an individual for use at his summer cottage, camp, etc., covers all liquor. This permit issued without charge to a holder of a general individual permit. Banquet permit, $2.00. Permits to druggists, dentists, physicians, certain manufacturers, hospitals, etc., 50 cents yearly. Priests and clergy permits, no fee.

SASKATCHEWAN—*Cont.*

No individual purchase permit system. Banquet permits issued—fee $2.00.

All purchases entered in permit holder's permit book. Purchases in any one day limited to 2 gals. (one case) of beer and 1 gal. of wine, and 55 ounces of any other liquor.

Daily limit to individuals not to exceed 2 gals. of beer and 1 gal. of wine and 1 qt. of any spirituous liquor. But provision is made to buy a larger quantity under special permit—$3.00 fee.

Government stores open 10 a.m. to 11 p.m. any day except Sunday. Closed Sundays, legal holidays and election days. No drinking in government stores.

All government stores open 11 a.m. to 7 or 8 p.m., also varying to provide for a weekly half holiday.

Beer sold at government stores by the bottle, carton or case. Beer by the glass sold in beer parlors, clubs, and beer parlors within hotels, the beer to be consumed within the room where sold. No food is sold in beer parlors, and no drinks excepting beer. The Act fixes the price of beer at not to exceed 10 cents a glass. Beer parlors place their order for beer with the Board accompanied by the cash. The Board then authorizes a brewer to deliver the beer to the beer parlor. Breweries deliver direct to permittees' residences under Board supervision. Imported beer and wine sold only in government stores.

Licensed beer and wine stores sell beer and native wine only and by the bottle only. No sale by the glass. Imported beer and wine sold only in government liquor stores.

Through government stores only—by the bottle.

Through government stores only—by the bottle.

NOVA SCOTIA—*Cont.*

ADVERTISING   Not allowed.

PROFITS   All profits from retail sales at government stores go direct to the Provincial Treasury.

TAXES EXCISE AND   No provincial tax on beer or liquor.
CUSTOMS DUTY

Note:—For information on federal (Dominion) customs and excise taxes see p. 122.

MANITOBA—*Cont.*

The Act allows liquor advertising but it is not done. Circularizing of permittees by brewers and distillers at their expense subject to Board censorship is allowed.

All profits from retail sales at government stores go direct to Provincial Treasury.

Manitoba brewers pay to the Board 12 ½¢ gal. tax on all beer sold within or without the Province. All outside brewers also pay to the Board 12½¢ cents gal. tax on beer sold in Manitoba.

Note:—For information on federal (Dominion) customs and excise taxes see p. 122.

SASKATCHEWAN—*Cont.*

Allowed only in newspapers, magazines, and year books—subject to approval of Board.

All profits from retail sales at government stores go direct to the Provincial Treasury.

No provincial tax on beer or liquor.

Note:—For information on federal (Dominion) customs and excise taxes see p. 122.

BRITISH COLUMBIA—
GOVERNMENT CONTROL

METHOD OF CONTROL	A Liquor Board—1 Commissioner at present—appointed by the Lieutenant-Governor-in-Council for indefinite period. The Board, at its own stores, makes retail sales, by the bottle, of spirituous liquor, wine, imported and British Columbia beer. No public drinking of spirituous liquor.
MANUFACTURE AND IMPORTATION	Manufacture in private hands, under federal license. Liquor Control Board alone may import.
WHOLESALE	All British Columbia sales by distilleries (operating under federal licenses) are made direct to the Board, which supplies the government stores from its own warehouses. No wholesale of beer or wine for consumption within British Columbia to other than the Board.
LOCAL OPTION	Applies only to beer parlors. The Board may establish stores wherever it deems advisable. Mail and express order purchases from head office permitted in local option areas.
LICENSES	All manufacturing is under federal control and taxation and subject to federal licensing. Special permits or licenses granted to druggists, physicians, hospitals, dentists, certain manufacturers, ministers, priests, etc. Breweries, distilleries, native wineries, all licensed by the Board. Hotels (beer parlors), clubs, veterans' organizations, all licensed to sell beer by the glass. Clubs are licensed to enable members to keep liquor therein for personal consumption, but not for sale. Veterans' clubs may sell only to their own members. All licenses expire December 31 of the year of issue.
PURCHASE CONDITIONS	One must obtain a permit to buy spirituous liquor, beer and wine—one permit covers all—yearly fee 25 cents.
AMOUNT ONE MAY BUY	All purchases recorded on permit holder's permit. No limit as to quantity of beer and liquor one may buy, but the vendor may exercise his discretion in the matter.

ONTARIO—
GOVERNMENT CONTROL

A Liquor Control Board consisting at present of 2 Commissioners appointed by the Lieutenant-Governor-in-Council—no fixed term. All retail sales of spirituous liquor, imported beer and wine made by the Board in its own stores—by the bottle. No sales by the glass—no public drinking.

Manufacture in private hands, with strict supervision by the Board of all wineries and breweries. Dominion Excise Department officials exercise strict supervision over distilleries. Liquor Control Board alone may import.

All provincial sales by the distilleries are made direct to the Board, which supplies the government retail stores from its own warehouses. No wholesale of beer or wine within the Province.

Much used feature of the Liquor Act. Mail and express order purchases from government stores permitted in local option areas.

All manufacturing is under federal control and taxation and subject to federal licensing. Special permits granted to druggists, physicians, hospitals, dentists, certain manufacturers, ministers, priests, etc. Brewers licensed by Board to keep for sale and sell beer to the Board and to permit holders. Distillers licensed to keep for sale and sell to the Board. Native wineries licensed by the Board to sell their products to the Board and direct to permit holders. All licenses or permits good for not exceeding 1 year. Permits granted by the Board for the sale of light beer.

One must obtain a permit in order to buy spirituous liquor, Ontario beer (excepting light beer—less than 2½% of alcohol), native wine: $2.00 a year for residents, $2.00 for non-residents (temporary—not over 1 month). Special permit, both resident and temporary, covering wine, native wine and beer, costs $1.00.

All purchases entered in permit holder's permit book, and the amount is subject to the discretion of the vendor or inspector. Maximum obtainable in one day, 1 case spirits, or 1 case wine, or 10 doz. qts., or 10 doz. pts., or ½ bbl., or two ¼ bbls., or four ⅛ bbls. of domestic beer.

BRITISH COLUMBIA—*Cont.*

HOURS OF SALE	General hours of liquor stores throughout British Columbia 10 a.m. to 6 p.m. Mon. to Fri., 12 noon to 8 p.m. Sat. In Vancouver one store open from 4 p.m. to 12 midnight (Sat. 3 p.m. to 11 p.m.). Beer parlors' hours vary—10 or 10:30 a.m. to 11 or 11:30 p.m., closed Sundays, certain holidays and election days.
HOW BEER AND WINES ARE SOLD	Beer sold by the glass, or by the bottle (for off-premises consumption) in licensed beer parlors. Brewers sell only to the Board, which in turn sells through its stores, to permit holders and licensees (beer parlors, clubs, etc.). Native wine sold only in government stores.
HOW DISTILLED SPIRITS ARE SOLD	Through government stores only—by the bottle.
ADVERTISING	Not allowed except in bona fide newspapers.
PROFITS	All profits from sales at government stores go direct to Provincial Treasury.
TAXES EXCISE AND CUSTOMS DUTY	All beer, wine and spirituous liquor, whether locally made or imported, pay no taxes in British Columbia. Note:—For information on federal (Dominion) customs and excise taxes see p. 122.

ONTARIO—*Cont.*

Generally speaking—10 a.m. to 6 p.m. each business day. Many stores close 1 p.m. Sat. Two Toronto stores and one in Ottawa 10 a.m. to 10 p.m. all business days (Sat. 7 p.m.). Few other stores 12 noon to 8 p.m. (Sat. 7 p.m.). Closed Sundays, legal holidays, election days.

Ontario beer and Ontario wine sold direct to the public by brewers from brewery plants and through brewers' warehouses and wineries, and from government stores. Imported beer and wine sold only in government stores. One or more Board officials are stationed in each brewery, brewer's warehouse and winery to supervise sales and endorse permits.

Through government stores only—by the bottle.

Not allowed.

All profits from retail sales at government stores go direct to Provincial Treasury.

On retail sales from breweries and brewers' warehouses, a 5% commission is levied by the Board. Provincial tax on domestic wine, 10¢ per gal. No provincial tax on domestic beer.

Note:—For information on federal (Dominion) customs and excise taxes see p. 122.

PRINCE EDWARD ISLAND has a prohibitory law, the sale of intoxicating liquor being under the control of a Board of Commissioners. A wholesale vendor is licensed to import and to sell to licensed retail vendors, who sell to those entitled to purchase, i.e., holders of physicians' prescriptions, and to holders of certificates to purchase for mechanical, pharmaceutical, hospital or such purposes. Vendors act as agents of the Board.

FEDERAL (DOMINION) CUSTOMS TAX ON:
> (1)   *Imported Spirituous Liquor* (From British countries)
> $8.00 per gal., 6% sales tax, 3% special excise tax, 18% on value of containers. (This amounts to about $9.00 per gal. on whiskey, gin, etc.—from non-British countries it would be about $10.25 per gal.)
>
> (2)   *Imported Beer* (From British countries)
> 30¢ per gal. customs duty, 12½¢ per gal. excise tax, 6% sales tax, 18% on value of containers. (This amounts to about 60¢ per gal.—from non-British countries it would be about 80¢ per gal.)
>
> (3)   *Wine*
> Import duty on wine varies with kind of wine, country of origin and alcoholic content.

FEDERAL (DOMINION) CUSTOMS EXCISE ON:
> (1)   *Domestic Spirituous Liquor*
> $7.00 per gal., 6% sales tax. (This amounts to about $5.50 to $6.00 per gal. on whiskey, gin, etc.)
>
> (2)   *Domestic Beer*
> 3¢ per lb. of malt, 12½¢ per gal. excise tax, 6% sales tax. (This amounts to about 26¢ per gal.)
>
> (3)   *Domestic Sparkling Wine*
> $1.50 per gal., 6% sales tax. (This amounts to about $1.85 per gal.)
>
> (4)   *Domestic Still Wine*
> 7½¢ per gal., 6% sales tax.

References above are to the Imperial gallon and, in respect to spirits, to a proof gallon; to bottled goods in cases (not bulk). The value on goods imported is the home consumption value in the country from which exported. Imports from British countries receive preferential treatment in customs rates.

HOW CERTAIN EUROPEAN COUNTRIES

NORWAY

METHOD OF CONTROL	Limited dividend company, the *Vinmonopolet*, privately owned, directed by Board of Directors of 5 members and 1 managing director appointed by the King. Powers relating to audit and to the framing of general policies repose in council of 15 members named by the *Storting* (parliament). Outside Oslo local boards serve in advisory capacity to the *Vinmonopolet* Board of Directors.
MANUFACTURE AND IMPORTATION	Private distillers produce raw spirits which may be sold only to *Vinmonopolet*, which in turn manufactures alcoholic beverages. Manufacture of beer and wine in private hands. *Vinmonopolet* alone may import.
WHOLESALE	Wholesale of wine and spirits entirely in hands of *Vinmonopolet*.
LOCAL OPTION	Municipal Councils under local option provisions may exclude sale of wine and spirits and may even place certain limitations on sale of beer.
LICENSES	Issuance of licenses determined by municipal councils. Licenses for consumption of spirits on premises are held in name of *Vinmonopolet* which appoints as its agents the managers of hotels and restaurants which serve spirits. Municipal licenses issued to restaurants and hotels to sell beer and wine.

APPENDIX III

H A N D L E   A L C O H O L I C   B E V E R A G E S

SWEDEN	ENGLAND
A private, limited dividend corporation, the *Vin & Spritcentralen*, under the Royal Board of Liquor Control appointed by the King, has control of importation, manufacture and wholesale trade in alcoholic beverages except beer. Retail sales by 122 other private limited-dividend system companies, each having 2 directors of its own choice, 2 appointed by local authorities and 1 by Royal Board. Characteristic feature— individual purchaser's pass book (*motbok*).	Licensing system. Licenses issued by justices appointed for life by the Lord Chancellor. Emphasis on limited hours of sale, reduction of number of licenses, increased taxation. State management of retail sale of alcoholic beverages exists in Carlisle and a small surrounding territory.
Distilled spirits manufactured by the *Vin & Spritcentralen* and by private producers who may sell only to the *Vin & Spritcentralen*. Swedish wine purchased from private manufacturers by the *Vin & Spritcentralen*. Manufacture of beer in private hands. *Vin & Spritcentralen* alone may import.	In private hands.
Wholesale of wine and spirits entirely in hands of *Vin & Spritcentralen*.	In private hands.
Local option privilege excludes all alcoholic beverages from some districts, wine and spirits from others. No prohibition on importation into dry areas.	Not a part of English system.
Licenses required for manufacture of beer, wine and spirits. Retail licenses required for restaurants and hotels selling wine and spirits for consumption on premises.	Distilleries, breweries, rectifiers, wineries are licensed. Retail licenses must be issued to individuals and also to premises where liquor is sold except theaters, registered clubs, premises of Ancient Vintners' Company, and shops selling exclusively by bottle for consumption off the premises. License for 1 year, may be extended to 7 years at discretion of justices.

NORWAY—*Cont.*

PURCHASE CONDITIONS	No personal purchase permit required. Purchaser must be twenty-one years of age.
AMOUNT ONE MAY BUY	No restriction on beer and wine. Reasonable amounts of spirits not questioned, except that sale is denied to persons reported by police or charity organization to be abusers.
HOURS OF SALE	*Vinmonopolet* stores for package sale open on ordinary days 11 a.m. to 5 p.m.; on Saturdays and days before holidays 11 a.m. to 1 p.m. except as these hours may be extended by municipal sanction; in Oslo hours on Saturdays and days before holidays are 9:30 a.m. to 1 p.m. For consumption on the premises the hours for wine are 8 a.m. to midnight; for spirits 3 p.m. to 11 p.m., except in large cities where municipal council may extend this to midnight.
HOW BEER AND WINES ARE SOLD	Beer up to 2.5% by weight sold without license or restrictions. License required for sale of heavier beer. Wine by bottle sold only at *Vinmonopolet* stores. Sale for consumption on premises by licensed restaurants and hotels.
HOW DISTILLED SPIRITS ARE SOLD	Spirits by bottle sold only by *Vinmonopolet* stores, by the glass only in restaurants and hotels appointed as agents of *Vinmonopolet* and limited in number by municipal council. Restricted as under "Hours of Sale."

SWEDEN—*Cont.*

One must obtain a pass book (*motbok*) in which all package purchases at System company shops are recorded.

Maximum purchase quota 4 liters (about 1.1 gal.) per month. Quotas of 1, 2 or 3 liters fixed for many. Quotas determined on basis of age, sex, whether head of household, financial condition and record of sobriety. No restriction on wine containing less than 14% alcohol, or beer, by the bottle. Amount of spirits and wine by glass determined by time of day and price of meal.

System company stores open 9 a.m. to 5 p.m. for bottle sale. Restaurants sell wine with food, 9 a.m. till 10 p.m.; spirits noon till 10 p.m.; some first-class restaurants till 1 a.m.

Retail sale of beer not restricted. Light wine under 14% not limited in amount but package purchases are recorded in pass book. Heavy wine over 14% restricted in amount; for consumption on premises restrictions depend on time of day and price of meal.

Spirits by bottle for consumption off premises sold by System companies only, each purchase recorded and limited (see above, "Amount One May Buy"). Spirits by glass sold with food, restricted in amount depending on time of day and price of meal.

ENGLAND—*Cont.*

No personal purchase permit required. Beer and cider may be sold with meals to persons over 16 years of age. Otherwise purchaser must be 18 years of age or over.

No restriction for liquor to be consumed off the premises, except one must buy not less than one pint of wine and not less than 1 quart of spirits. For consumption on premises purchases may be by glass or bottle.

Permitted hours: London, weekdays, 9 hours between 11 a.m. and 11 p.m., with break of 2 hours some time after 12 noon. Sundays and certain holidays, 5 hours, only 2 of these between 12 noon and 3 p.m.; not more than 3 between 6 p.m. and 10 p.m. Other parts of England; week-days, 8 hours with same 2-hour break; Sundays and holidays, same as London.

In public houses ("pubs"), restaurants and hotels by the glass; in shops by the bottle.

Same as beer and wine.

NORWAY—*Cont.*

ADVERTISING

Vinmonopolet does not advertise. Agents of foreign manufacturers may advertise.

PROFITS

Excess profits over the 5% permitted to shareholders go to state.

TAXES EXCISE AND
CUSTOMS DUTY

Beer subject to manufacturers' tax.
Wines and spirits subject to import duty, manufacturers' tax and 25% on turnover of spirits.

SWEDEN—*Cont.*

Self-imposed restrictions by monopoly sales companies.

Excess profits over fixed dividends (6% for *Vin & Spritcentralen*, 5% for the 122 System companies) accrue to state.

Beer subject to manufacturers' tax.
Malt tax.

Manufacturing tax on domestic brandy or *brännvin*.
Customs duty on spirits and wine.
Tax on spirits sold by glass.
Tax on turnover of all spirits, 60% of amount paid by System companies for all spirits.

ENGLAND—*Cont.*

Not restricted.

Private profit, not limited by government.
In Carlisle profits go to government.

Beer. Subject to customs duty per barrel; also excise rate varying with specific gravity of the beer.
Wine. Wine in casks subject to customs duty varying with alcoholic content. Wine in bottles, in addition to customs duty above, subject to gallonage tax. No excise.
Spirits. Customs and excise on spirits per proof gallon.

APPENDIX III

HOW   CERTAIN   EUROPEAN   COUNTRIES

HOLLAND

METHOD OF CONTROL	Licensing system. The provincial government issues "full licenses" for on- and off-premises consumption. Retail licenses for bottle sale issued by burgomaster and aldermen of the municipality. Licenses limited in number in proportion to population, in ratios varying with size of city.
MANUFACTURE AND IMPORTATION	In private hands.
WHOLESALE	In private hands. No license. No restriction.
LOCAL OPTION	Provision that every 5 years municipal council may petition Crown for reduction in licenses issued by provincial government; decision by Ministry of Interior, effective by Royal decree. Municipalities may set aside geographical areas where there may be no licenses.
LICENSES	Retail licenses issued by burgomaster of the town or city, fee based on rental value of property. Registration permits but not licenses required to sell beer and wine or spirits under 15% alcoholic content, by bottle. Licenses are of 3 classes: (1) for sale of beer and wine for consumption on premises; (2) for sale of spirits by bottle for consumption off the premises; (3) for sale of spirits for consumption on the premises. A "full license" permits sale for consumption both on and off the premises.
PURCHASE CONDITIONS	No personal purchase permit required. Those under 16 not permitted to enter licensed places.

H A N D L E   A L C O H O L I C   B E V E R A G E S

RUSSIA

State Alcohol Monopoly has exclusive right to handle all products of state, coöperative and private plants. Liquor sold at retail at government stores for consumption off premises; at hotels and restaurants for consumption on premises. Emphasis on temperance education.

Vodka made by state monopoly only. Other alcohol may be made by state, coöperative or private plants.

Under state control.

Demands for discontinuing sale of vodka in various districts are complied with. Any local store may be closed by government, depending on local conditions.

Government controlled, with policy of progressive decrease in number of licensed places. Distribution restricted as far as possible to government stores.

No personal purchase permit required. Purchaser must be 18 years of age.

FINLAND

Control is by the Alcohol Company which is state owned and operated. Board of Control consists of 7 regular and 3 deputy members named by Cabinet. This Board is responsible for policies; its business management is under Board of Directors appointed by Board of Control.

Manufacture of beer by private interests; manufacture and import of other alcoholic beverages in hands of Alcohol Company.

By the Alcohol Company.

Local sentiment is sought and considered in licensing shops.

Hotels and restaurants are licensed by governors of Provinces. All other licenses are issued by Alcohol Company which takes local sentiment into account in licensing and in opening shops.

No personal purchase permit required. Hotels and restaurants may not serve liquor to anyone under 18 years of age. Purchaser by bottle at stores must be not obviously under 21.

HOLLAND—*Cont.*

AMOUNT ONE MAY BUY	No restriction in amount, but purchases of over 10 liters must be made from wholesale establishment.
HOURS OF SALE	Some licensed premises are open as early as 6 a.m. and as late as 12:30 a.m.
HOW BEER AND WINES ARE SOLD	By the bottle without license. For consumption on premises by licensed places.
HOW DISTILLED SPIRITS ARE SOLD	For consumption both on and off the premises by licensees. Hotels may sell only to guests.
ADVERTISING	Not restricted.
PROFITS	Private profit not limited by government.
TAXES EXCISE AND CUSTOMS DUTY	Beer, wines and spirits subject to manufacturers' tax and to import duty, both varying with alcoholic content, and to a tax on turnover.

RUSSIA—*Cont.*	FINLAND—*Cont.*
Liquor with alcoholic content of more than 40% limited to one bottle at one time.	At stores for consumption off the premises: 2 liters of spirits, 5 liters of wine, 20 liters of beer at any time at any shop. More may be had for special occasions, subject to approval by shop manager.
No sale on holidays or pay days. Local authorities may establish other restrictions.	Shops open 10 a.m. to 5 p.m. every day except Sundays, holidays and days preceding a few holidays, e.g., Christmas, May 1, June 23.
Beer in beer parlors. Beer and wine by bottle in government stores; for consumption on premises by hotels and restaurants.	Beer under 2.25% sold without restriction; beer over 2.25% sold through Alcohol Company. Class B² restaurants sell only wine and beer. Class C restaurants sell only beer.
By bottle in government stores; for consumption on premises in hotels and restaurants.	Same as beer and wine, in Company stores by bottle. Class A restaurants sell all beverages. Class B restaurants sell all beverages up to 21%, and over 21% if blended with water. Aquavit sold only with meals, amount limited.
Not permitted.	Alcohol Company does not advertise.
Profits of state alcohol monopoly go to state.	Profits of Alcohol Company belong to state.
Alcoholic beverages subject ot a liter tax and to tax based on alcoholic content.	Beer up to 1.8% alcoholic content tax free. Other beer taxed at rates varying with alcoholic content. Duties levied on all alcoholic beverages imported. Alcohol Company pays local and national taxes on same basis as other business concerns.

APPENDIX IV

EXPLANATORY NOTES AND DEFINITIONS

ALCOHOL

Alcohol as it is produced in its pure state is known as ethyl alcohol or ethanol. Ethyl alcohol was generally referred to some years ago as "grain alcohol" because it was made largely from grain. The term is today practically a misnomer, as 90 per cent of all alcohol is now made from molasses.

Denatured alcohol is ethyl alcohol to which have been added such denaturing materials as render the alcohol unfit for use as a beverage.

All alcohol producing plants in the United States are privately owned, but are operated under government permit and supervision. The permits are granted after an investigation is made of the officers and stockholders of the corporation, the source of the capital invested, the construction of the plant and the process of manufacture.

Federal inspectors known as "storekeeper gaugers" are constantly on duty and supervise all manufacture, storage and shipment of alcohol and the keeping of records.

Each alcohol distillery is heavily bonded, and the federal government obtains a prior lien on the property which is liable to forfeiture on proof of violation of the law and regulations governing plant operation.[1]

ALCOHOLIC BEVERAGES

The alcoholic beverages commonly made and consumed contain up to 45 per cent of alcohol by weight. They are grouped into three classes, based on their process of manufacture:

    (a) The FERMENTED BEVERAGES comprising beer, cider, wine and kindred products, characterized by an alcoholic content of less than 12 per cent by weight.

    (b) The DISTILLED SPIRITS such as gin, brandy, whiskey and rum containing more than 24 per cent alcohol.

    (c) MIXTURES which include fortified wines and liqueurs combining the characteristics of the two above major groups and containing from 12 to 35 per cent of alcohol by weight.

The Fermented Beverages are subdivided into two major classifications which are:

    (a) Beer and Ale.

    (b) Wine, Vinous Products and Cider.

The differentiation between these two groups of fermented products is based on the raw material. Beers are made from grains, while wines, vinous products and ciders are made from fruit juices.

BEERS AND ALES. Beers and ales are made from malted barley, cereals, hops and water. The grains are mashed and cooked in water and the liquid containing the starches, converted into soluble sugar, is separated from the spent grain. This solution called "wort" is flavored with hops and fermented by the addition of yeast, which produces the green beer. This green beer is aged before sending it out to the trade. The process of brewing is standardized by modern factory methods and lasts from one to four months.

---

[1] "Industrial Alcohol." United States Treasury Department, 1930.

Beers and ales contain water from 85 to 92 per cent, solid material from 4 to 8 per cent, alcohol from 2 to 6 per cent and carbonic acid about one-half of 1 per cent by weight. The solids are sugars, proteins, and mineral salts such as phosphates and potash. All beers possess definite food value on account of their sugars and their alcohol and these foods are in a readily assimilable form. The most distinctive characteristic of beer is its foamy head, which is due mostly to the carbonic acid.

WINE is the naturally fermented product of the grape. Similar products are also made from other fruits, e.g., cider from apples, perry from pears, and date and fig wine, etc. The numerous varieties of grapes supply the raw material for over 95 per cent of the wines made in the whole world.

The process of manufacture is simple. The grapes are crushed and the juice is pressed out. This juice is called "must." It is fermented and the resultant green wine is aged, blended and prepared for the trade. For quality products, aging takes one year or more.

Naturally fermented wines contain from 5 to 12 per cent of alcohol by weight, 1 to 4 per cent of solids, 80 to 90 per cent of water. Wine has food value, by virtue of its alcoholic content, the unfermented sugars and the acids produced during the manufacturing and ageing processes

DISTILLED SPIRITS. Alcohol in concentrations greater than 12 per cent by weight are rarely produced by fermentation. If greater concentrations of alcohol are desired, it is necessary to distil or separate the alcohol from the mother-solutions and to condense the alcohol vapors. The result is called DISTILLED SPIRITS, and these have to be rectified, cured, aged and processed to become beverages. They are sold under the names of gin, brandy, whiskey, rum, etc. These various products are distinguished by the raw materials used in their manufacture. Brandy uses wine as a raw material, while whiskey is made from fermented grains and rum from molasses. Distilled liquors have no food value other than the alcohol they contain, and the flavors readily hide the unpalatable quality of this major ingredient.

MIXTURES are those alcoholic beverages made by combining fermented and distilled spirits. The *fortified wines* containing from 12 to 18 per cent alcohol, such as port, sherry, tonics, medicated drinks, are made from a wine base with brandy additions. The *liqueurs* contain large amounts of sugars, flavors and herb extracts (10 to 20 per cent), besides 25 to 45 per cent of alcohol by volume.

PROOF-SPIRIT

Proof-Spirit: A term adopted to indicate the standard by which the strength, or alcoholic content, of distilled products is measured for revenue purposes. The word "proof" refers exclusively to strength and implies nothing whatever as regards the purity of the liquid.

English proof-spirit: In England, proof-spirit must have alcohol 12/13 the weight of an equal volume of distilled water at 51° F. That is to say, 100° English proof-spirit contains 49.3 per cent *by weight* of absolute alcohol.

United States proof-spirit: In the United States, spirits are said to be proof when one-half the volume is alcohol at 60° F. and of a specific gravity of 0.7939. The highest degree of proof is 200° which is absolute alcohol (ethyl), or 100 per cent alcohol by volume. A liquid is said to be 100-proof when it is 50 per cent alcohol by volume. The simple term "proof-spirits" is often used to mean 100 proof spirits, containing 50 per cent alcohol by volume.

MEASURES

Gallon: United States standard gallon is 231 cubic inches. The British Imperial gallon is 277.274 cubic inches.

A wine gallon is a measure of liquid quantity of any proof, i.e., in the United States a wine gallon is the regular liquid measure of 231 cubic inches of liquid of any proof; in Great Britain a wine gallon is 277.274 cubic inches of liquid of any proof.

A proof gallon is a wine gallon of 100 per cent proof-spirits, i.e., it is 50 per cent alcohol by volume. A wine gallon of 200 proof (the highest proof), which is absolute alcohol or 100 per cent by volume would, therefore, be equivalent to two proof or tax gallons.

Industrial alcohol as generally produced ranges from 188 to 192 proof.

A wine gallon of alcohol as usually produced, averaging 190 proof, would be almost two (1.9) proof gallons. The fact should, therefore, be kept in mind that a wine gallon is almost twice the volume of a 100-proof or tax gallon, or, stated the other way around, a tax gallon is almost half the volume of a wine gallon. Records of production and disposition in statistical tables show distilled (except denatured) alcohol in tax or proof gallons. To give a concrete example: a whiskey 50 per cent alcohol by volume is 100 proof. One wine gallon of this liquor would, therefore, be equivalent to one proof or tax gallon. A whiskey with alcoholic content of 53 per cent by volume is 106 proof and a wine gallon of this would be the equivalent of 1.06 proof or tax gallons and would, therefore, be taxed on that basis.

United States Government statistical tables show wines, beers and denatured alcohol in wine gallons for revenue purposes.

Alcohol by weight ahd by volume: A calculation of alcohol by weight can be converted to a calculation of alcohol by volume, and vice versa as follows:

Alcohol by weight = alcohol by volume multiplied by .80.

Alcohol by volume = alcohol by weight multiplied by 1.25.

APPENDIX V

PERCENTAGE OF ABSOLUTE ALCOHOL IN VARIOUS BEVERAGES

			1.00	.80
Per Cent by Volume			1.00	.80
Per Cent by Weight			1.25	1.00

CLASSIFICATION	BEVERAGE	U.S.A. PROOF	% BY VOL.	% BY WT.
Beers—Light..............	Light Beer (local	...	3.00	2.40
	1933 Legal American Beer	...	4.00	3.20
	German Beer Most Largely Used ..	...	4.38	3.50
—Strong...........	Export Lager	...	5.00	4.00
	Ale and Porter	...	6.25	5.00
Ciders	Barrel Cider.................................	...	3.50	2.80
	Bottled Cider	...	6.00	4.80
Wines	Moselle...	...	6.65	5.10
	Rhine; Claret	...	9.62	7.70
	Bordeaux (White, Red)	...	11.50	9.20
	Chianti; Muscatel	...	12.50	10.00
	California—average.......................	...	11.30	8.80
	Burgundy......................................	...	13.50	10.80
Sparkling Wines	Sparkling—average.......................	...	8.50	6.80
	Mousseaux	...	10.00	8.00
	Champagne	...	12.50	10.00
Fortified Wines...........	Proprietary Medicines...................		16.00	12.80
	Port and Sherry		19.00	16.20
	Medicated Wines (Tonics)		22.00	17.60
Liqueurs	Chartreuse	64	32.00	25.60
	Benedictine	84	42.00	33.60
	Cointreau......................................	80	40.00	32.00
	Absinthe	110	55.00	42.40
Whiskey	Gin..	70	35.00	27.00
	Cognac	90	45.00	35.00
	Brandy Gin...................................	80	40.00	32.00
	Whiskey—common	86	43.00	34.40
	Brandy Gin—heavy	94	47.00	37.60
	American Whiskey—best	100	50.00	40.00
	Rum..	110	55.00	44.00

APPENDIX VI

SELECTED BIBLIOGRAPHY

Alcohol: A Review of the Effects of Alcohol on Man. London: Victor Gollancz, Ltd., 1931. Pp. 300.

Alcohol: The Social and Economic Aspects of the Drink Problem. London: Victor Gollancz, Ltd., 1931, Pp. 180.

Annals of the American Academy of Political and Social Science, The. Philadelphia:
Johnson, Emory R. (Editor): "Regulation of the Liquor Traffic." Vol. XXXII, No. 3, November, 1908. Pp. iii + 172.
Walnut, Henry T. (Editor): "Prohibition and Its Enforcement." Vol. CIX, No. 198, September, 1923. Pp. iv + 285.
Bossard, James H. S., and Sellin, Thorsten (Editors): "Prohibition: A National Experiment." Vol. 163, September, 1932. Pp. v + 269.

Anti-Saloon League Year Book, The. Cherrington, E. H. (Compiler and Editor). Westerville, Ohio: The American Issue Press, 1908 to date. See also other publications of the same organization.

Askwith, Lord: *British Taverns; Their History and Laws*. London: George Routledge Sons, Ltd., 1928. Pp. 274.

Barker, John Marshall: *The Saloon Problem and Social Reform*. Boston: The Everett Press, 1905. Pp. vii + 212.

Barnes, Harry Elmer: *Prohibition versus Civilization; Analyzing the Dry Psychosis*. New York: The Viking Press, 1932. Pp. 127.

Beman, Lamar T.: *Selected Articles on Prohibition; Modification of the Volstead Law*. New York: The H. W. Wilson Co., 1924. Pp. lxxi + 380.

Binkley, Robert Cedric: *Responsible Drinking; A Discreet Inquiry and a Modest Proposal*. New York: The Vanguard Press, 1930. Pp. viii + 215.

Blakey, Leonard Stott: *The Sale of Liquor in the South*. New York: Columbia University, 1912. Pp. 56.

British Journal of Inebriety. T. N. Kelynack (Editor). Quarterly. London: Balliére, Tindall and Cox, 1903 to date. See also, periodical publications of various interest groups in all countries.

Bruére, Martha Bensley: *Does Prohibition Work?* New York: Harper and Bros., 1927. Pp. vii + 329.

Cambiaire, Célestin Pierre: *The Black Horse of the Apocalypse; (Wine, Alcohol and Civilization)*. Paris: J. Gamber, 1932. Pp. xii +486.

Carter, Henry: *The Control of the Drink Trade in Great Britain; A Contribution to National Efficiency During the Great War, 1915-1918*. 2nd ed. London: Longmans, Green and Co., 1919. Pp. xix + 343.

Carver, Thomas Nixon: *Government Control of the Liquor Business in Great Britain and the United States*. New York: Carnegie Endowment for International Peace, 1919. Pp. v + 192.

Catlin, George E. G.: *Liquor Control*. New York: Henry Holt & Co., Inc., 1931. Pp. 259.

Cherrington, Ernest H.: *The Evolution of Prohibition in the United States of America*. Westerville, Ohio: The American Issue Press, 1920. Pp. 384.

Colvin, D. Leigh: *Prohibition in the United States; A History of the Prohibition Party and of the Prohibition Movement*. New York: George H. Doran Co., 1926. Pp. x + 678.

Committee of Fifty Investigation of the Liquor Problem. Boston and New York: Houghton Mifflin Co., 6 vols., 1893-1905.

Wines, Frederic H., and Koren, John: *The Liquor Problem in Its Legislative Aspects*. 2nd ed., 1898. Pp. viii + 425.

Koren, John: *Economic Aspects of the Liquor Problem*. 1899. Pp. x + 327.

Calkins, Raymond: *Substitutes for the Saloon*, 1901. Pp. xvi + 397.

Billings, John S. (Editor): *Physiological Aspects of the Liquor Problem*. 2 vols., 1903. I, pp. xxii + 396; II, pp. 379.

The Liquor Problem; A Summary of Investigations Conducted by the Committee of Fifty 1893-1903, 1905. Pp. ix + 182.

Darrow, Clarence and Yarros, Victor S.: *The Prohibition Mania*. New York: Boni and Liveright, 927. Pp. vii + 254.

Debar, Joseph (Compiler): *Prohibition; Its Relation to Temperance, Good Morals and Sound Government*. Cincinnati, circa 1910. Pp. 311.

Dodge, Raymond and Benedict, Francis, G.: *Psychological Effects of Alcohol; An Experimental Investigation of the Effects of Moderate Doses of Ethyl Alcohol on a Related Group of Neuromuscular Processes in Man*. Washington: Carnegie Institution of Washington Publication No. 232, 1915. Pp. 281.

Dorchester, Daniel: *The Liquor Problem in All Ages*. New York: Phillips and Hunt, 1884. Pp. 656.

Dorr, Rheta Childe: *Drink: Coercion or Control?* New York: Frederick A. Hollis Co., 1929. Pp. 330.

Eddy, Richard: *Alcohol in History*. Mauston, Wis.: Good Templars, 1888. Pp. xii + 481.

Emerson, Haven (Editor) *Alcohol and Man; The Effects of Alcohol on Man in Health and Disease*. New York: The Macmillan Co., 1932. Pp. xi + 451.

Feldman, Herman: *Prohibition—Its Economic and Industrial Aspects*. New York: D. Appleton and Co., 1928. Pp. xv + 415.

Fisher, Irving (assisted by) Brougham, H. Bruce: *Prohibition Still At Its Worst*. 1928. Pp. xxvii + 358; *The "Noble Experiment."* 1930 Pp. xliv + 493. New York: The Alcohol Information Committee. See also, other publications of the same organization.

Flint, George Elliot: *The Whole Truth About Alcohol*. New York: The Macmillan Co., 1919. Pp. xii + 294.

French, Richard Valpey: *Nineteen Centuries of Drink in England*. 2nd ed., revised. London: National Temperance Publication Depot, 1891. Pp. xx + 398.

Gebhart, John C. (Director of Research Dept.) *The Quebec System; A Study in Liquor Control*. Washington: Association Against the Prohibition Amendment, 2nd ed., June, 1930. Pp. 43. See also, other publications of the same organization.

Gordon, Ernest: *When the Brewer Had the Stranglehold*. New York: Alcohol Information Committee, 1930. Pp. ix + 276.

Gordon, Leslie (Director and Editor) Jackson-Babbitt Inc. (Compiler): *The New Crusade Including a Report Concerning Prohibition and Fifteen Centuries of Liquor Legislation*. Cleveland: The Crusaders Inc., 1932. Pp. xxxix + 283.

Great Britain Government Publications.

Royal Commission on Licensing (England and Wales) 1929-31 Report. London: H. M. Stationery Office, 1932. Pp. vii + 307.

Central Control Board (Liquor Traffic). *Advisory Committee. Alcohol: Its Action on the Human Organism.* 2nd ed., revised. London: H. M. Stationery Office, 1924. Pp. xx + 170. Reprinted in U. S. Senate Report No. 1105, 72nd Congress, 2nd Session. Washington: Government Printing Office, 1933.

Gunther, Konrad: *Prohibition in Its True Emplacement.* New York: Walter Neale, 1931. Pp. 236.

Hose, Reginald E.: *Prohibition or Control? Canada's Experience With the Liquor Problem 1921-1927.* New York: Longmans, Green and Co., 1928. Pp. viii + 132.

Joint Committee on Health Problems in Education, Report. 2nd ed. (revised and enlarged with the coöperation of the Technical Committee of Fifty). New York: The National Education Association and The American Medical Association with the Coöperation of the Technical Committee of Twenty-seven, 1930. 2nd printing 1931. Pp. 251.

Jones, Robert L.: *The Eighteenth Amendment and Our Foreign Relations.* New York: Thomas Y. Crowell Co., 1933. Pp. vii + 192.

Koren, John: *Alcohol and Society.* New York: Henry Holt and Co., 1916. Pp. vi + 271.

Kelynack, T. N. (Editor) *The Drink Problem of Today; In Its Medico-Sociological Aspects.* London: Methuen and Co., Ltd., 1916. Pp. xii + 318.

Lewis, Elmer A. (Compiler) *Liquor Laws.* (Federal) Washington: Government Printing Office, 1932. Pp. 72.

Matthai, John: *Excise and Liquor Control.* Madras: The Authors Press and Publishing House, 1924. Pp. 88.

Mencken, Percival S.: *Regulation of the Liquor Traffic.* New York: Columbia College, 1891. Pp. 77.

Merz, Charles: *The Dry Decade.* New York: Doubleday, Doran and Co., 1932. Pp. 343.

Miles, Walter R.: *Effect of Alcohol on Psycho-Physiological Functions.* Washington: Carnegie Institution Publication No. 266, 1918. Pp. 144; *Alcohol and Human Efficiency, Experiments With Moderate Quantities and Dilute Solutions of Ethyl Alcohol on Human Subjects.* Washington: Carnegie Institution Publication No. 333, 1924. Pp. x + 298.

Mitchell, Kate: *The Drink Question; Its Social and Medical Aspects.* London: Swan Sonnenchein and Co., *circa* 1890. Pp. 254.

Moehlman, Conrad Henry: *When All Drank and Thereafter.* New York: Alcohol Information Committee, 1930. Pp. x + 149.

Monahan, M. (Editor) *A Textbook of True Temperance.* 2nd ed., revised. New York: United States Brewers' Association, 1911. Pp. 323.

Moray, Alastair: *The Diary of a Rum Runner.* London: Philip Allan and Co., Ltd., 1929. Pp. xiv + 272.

Münsterberg, Hugo:" Prohibition and Temperance" and "The Intemperance of Women" in *American Problems*, Pp. 69-113. New York: Moffat, Yard and Co., 1912.

Odegard, Peter H.: *Pressure Politics; The Story of the Anti-Saloon League.* New York: Columbia University Press, 1928. Pp. x + 299.

Partridge, G. E.: *Studies in the Psychology of Intemperance.* New York: Sturgis and Walton Co., 1912. Pp. 275.

Peabody, Richard R.: *The Common Sense of Drinking.* Boston: Little, Brown and Co., 1931. Pp. xvi + 191.

Pearl, Raymond: *Alcohol and Longevity.* New York: Alfred A. Knopf, 1926. Pp. xii + 273.

Reeves, Ira L. : *Ol' Rum River; Revelations of a Prohibition Administrator*. Chicago: Thomas S. Rockwell Co., 1931. Pp. xii + 383.

Root, Grace C.: *Thirty Seven Liquor Control Systems of Today*. October, 1932. Pp. 50; *More Liquor Control Systems of Today*. March, 1933. Pp. 49. New York: The Women's Organization for National Prohibition Reform. See also, other publications of the same organization.

Ross, E. B.: *Government Sale of Liquor in Canada; Ten Years' Experience*. Seattle: Lex Publishing Co., 1932. Pp. 130.

Rowntree, Joseph and Sherwell, Arthur: *The Temperance Problem and Social Reform*. 7th ed. New York: Truslove Hanson and Comba, 1900. Pp. xxxi + 777. Also, 9th ed.

Rowntree, Joseph, and Sherwell, Arthur: *The Taxation of the Liquor Trade*. Vol. I, "Public Houses, Hotels, Restaurants, Theatres, Railway Bars and Clubs." 2nd ed. London: Macmillan and Co., Ltd., 1908. Pp. xxviii + 575.

Schmeckebier, Laurence F.: "The Bureau of Prohibition; Its History, Activities and Organization." *Service Monographs of the U. S. Government, No. 57*. Washington: The Brookings Institution, 1929. Pp. x + 333.

Selley, Ernest: *The English Public House As It Is*. London: Longmans, Green and Co., Ltd., 1927. Pp. v + 184.

Shadwell, Arthur: *Drink, Temperance and Legislation*. 1902. Pp. x + 304; *Drink in 1914-1922; A Lesson in Control*. 1923. Pp. xi + 245. London: Longmans, Green & Co., Ltd.

Sites, Clement Moore Lacey: *Centralized Administration of Liquor Laws in the American Commonwealths*. New York: Columbia University Press, 1899. Pp. xii + 162.

Smith, Sydney: "Alcohol and Behavior." *The Henderson Trust Lectures, No. X*. Edinburgh: Oliver and Boyd, Ltd., 1930. Pp. 37.

Spence, Ruth Elizabeth: *Prohibition in Canada*. Toronto: Dominion Alliance, 1919. Pp. xvi + 624.

Social Science Research Council, A Report of a Special Advisory Committee: *Sources of Information Concerning the Operation of the Eighteenth Amendment*. (Mimeographed) New York, 1928. Pp. 70.

Standard Encyclopedia of the Alcohol Problem. E. H. Cherrington (Editor-in-Chief) 6 vols. Westerville, Ohio: American Issue Publishing Co., 1925-1930. See also, other encyclopædias under relevant headings: *Britannica; New International; Bliss' New Encyclopedia of Social Reform; The Encyclopædia of the Social Sciences* and *The Cyclopædia of Temperance and Prohibition*. (Funk, 1891.)

Starcke, J.: *Alcohol: The Sanction for Its Use*. Translated from the German. New York: G. P. Putnam's Sons, 1910. Pp. xx + 317.

Starling, Ernest H., *et al.*: *The Action of Alcohol on Man*. London: Longmans, Green and Co., 1923. Pp. vi + 291.

Sullivan, W. C.: *Alcoholism; A Chapter in Social Pathology*. London: James Nisbet and Co., 1906. Pp. vi + 214.

Thomann, Gallus: *Documentary History of the United States Brewers' Association*. Parts I and II. New York: U. S. Brewers' Association, 1896. Pp. 477.

Tillitt, Malvern Hall: *The Price of Prohibition*. New York: Harcourt, Brace and Co., 1932. Pp. xvii + 156.

Tydings, Millard E.: *Before and After Prohibition*. New York: The Macmillan Co., 1930. Pp. ix + 131.

United States Government Publications.

Amendment of the Prohibition Act. Hearings Before a Subcommittee of the Committee on Manufacture. U. S. Senate. 72nd Congress, 1st Session on S. 436 "A Bill to Amend the National Prohibition Act, As Amended and Supplemented, In Respect to the Definition of Intoxicating Liquor" and S. 2473 "A Bill to Provide for Increasing the Permissible Alcoholic Content of Beer, Ale, or Porter to 3 ²⁄₁₀ per centum by Weight and to Provide Means By Which All Such Beer, Ale, or Porter Shall Be Made of Products of American Farms." January 8 to February 19, 1932. Washington: Government Printing Office, 1932. Pp. iii + 574.

Bureau of Prohibition:

Digest of Various State Laws Relating to the Manufacture, Sale, Importation, Exportation, and Transportation of Beverages Containing Not More Than 3.2 Per Centum of Alcohol by Weight. Washington: (Mimeographed) July 15, 1933. Pp. 42.

Alcohol, Hygiene and the Public Schools; Digest of State Laws. Washington: Division of Research and Public Information, 1931. Pp. 44. See also, other publications of the Bureau of Prohibition.

National Commission on Law Observance and Enforcement.

George W. Wickersham, Chairman:

Report on the Enforcement of the Prohibition Laws of the United States. No. 2. Also, 71st Congress, 3rd Session; House Document No. 722. Washington: Government Printing Office, 1931. Pp. viii + 162.

Enforcement of the Prohibition Laws. Official Records of the National Commission on Law Observance and Enforcement Pertaining to Its Investigation of the Facts as to the Enforcement, the Benefits, and the Abuses Under the Prohibition Laws, Both Before and Since the Adoption of the Eighteenth Amendment to the Constitution. 5 vols. 71st Congress, 3rd Session; Senate Document No. 307. Washington: Government Printing Office, 1931. Pp. I, iii + 460; II, 399; III, 364; IV, 1176; V, 761.

The National Prohibition Law; Hearings Before the Subcommittee of the Committee on the Judiciary. U. S. Senate. 69th Congress, 1st Session on S. 33, S. 34, S. 591, S. 592, S. 3118, S.J.Res. 34, S.J.Res. 81, S.J.Res. 85, S. 3823, S. 3411, and S. 3891 "Bills to Amend the National Prohibition Act." April 5 to 24, 1926, 2 vols. Washington: Government Printing Office, 1926. Pp. vii + 1660.

Treasury Department; Bureau of Internal Revenue: Prohibition Unit 1924-1927; Bureau of Prohibition 1928-1930; Bureau of Industrial Alcohol 1930-1932. *Statistics Concerning Intoxicating Liquors.* Washington: Government Printing Office; Date and Pages: (May) 1924, v + 33; (April) 1925, iv + 38; (March) 1926, iv + 51; (Feb.) 1927, iv + 53; (April) 1928, iv + 51; (Feb.) 1929, iv + 57; (Jan.) 1930, iv + 73; (Dec.) 1930, ii + 84; (Dec.) 1931, iv + 99; (Dec.) 1932, vii + 149.

United Sates Brewers' Association Year Book. New York, 1909-1923. See also, other publications of the same organization.

Vecki, Victor G.: *Alcohol and Prohibition in Their Relation to Civilization and the Art of Living.* Philadelphia: J. B. Lippincott Co., 1923. Pp. ix + 165.

Vernon, H. M.: *The Alcohol Problem.* London: Balliére, Tindall and Cox, 1928. Pp. xv + 252.

Warburton, Clark: *The Economic Results of Prohibition.* New York: Columbia University Press, 1932. Pp. 273.

Warner, Harry S.: *Social Welfare and the Liquor Problem*. Chicago: The Intercollegiate Prohibition Association, 1909. Pp. 274.

Webb, Sidney and Beatrice: *The History of Liquor Licensing in England Principally from 1700 to 1830*. London: Longmans, Green and Co., 1903. Pp. ix + 162.

Weeks, Courtenay C.: *Alcohol and Human Life*. London: H. K. Lewis and Co., Ltd. 1929. Pp. x + 201.

Winskill, P. T.: *The Temperance Movement and Its Workers*. 4 vols. London: Blackie and Son, Ltd., 1892. I, xxvii + 259; II, viii + 292; III, viii + 288; IV, viii + 288.

Wuorinen, John H.: *The Prohibition Experiment in Finland*. New York: Columbia University Press, 1931. Pp. x + 251.

INDEX

EDITOR'S NOTE

AN EDITOR OF AN UNABRIDGED BOOK SUCH AS THIS REALLY DOES NOT have much to do, especially with a book as important and well-researched as *Toward Liquor Control* by Raymond Fosdick and Albert Scott.

This book speaks for itself, so the job here is to shine a light on this work that is a blueprint for how governments can solve thorny alcohol policy issues. This book provides guidelines for how to regulate a socially sensitive product like alcohol and the industry that profits from it. The goal of this re-print is not to change what was written nor shape your perspective. It simply is to advance the education started by the authors in 1933.

The only changes that have been made to *Toward Liquor Control* are the addition of this editor's note and an introduction by five leading voices of alcohol regulation. I will defer to another day a project to produce an abridged or annotated version of this book, including the various methods states have specifically adopted to effectuate the authors' goal of temperance. The authors wisely predicted a wide variety of approaches to regulating alcohol by the states noting that "the forty-eight states will constitute a social science laboratory in which different ideas and methods can be tested, and the exchange of experience will be infinitely valuable for the future."

This project would not have happened without the leadership and support of the Center for Alcohol Policy and its commitment to serving as the preeminent thought leader for discussions of alcohol policy and regulation.

Specific recognition must be given to Amy Foster and Kelsey Lamb for their attention to and patience for this project. Moreover, the work of Webster, Chamberlain & Bean, the staffs of the National Beer Wholesalers Association and Bedwick & Jones Printing were critical for this project's success. Finally, I would like to thank the Rockefeller Foundation, Mr. Stephen F. Downs, Mrs. Elinor Fosdick Downs, and Harper Publishing for their assistance in bringing this important document back into circulation.

Paul Pisano
Senior Vice President & General Counsel,
National Beer Wholesalers Association